ACHIEVING
LIFE & CAREER SUCCESS
Workbook

7

SEVEN STEPS

Odyssey of
Learning

Cloud of
Unknowing

Creative
Visualization

Attitudes
Disciplines

Your Ten
Year Goals

Your Path
of Life

Define
Success

By Dennis J. Sobotka

Email: achievingsuccesscenter@gmail.com
Website: www.achievingsuccesscenter.com

Paperback Version
ISBN 978-0-9969083-5-1

Buffalo, New York
Published by Achieving Success Press
Email: achievingsuccesscenter@gmail.com
Website: www.achievingsuccesscenter.com

DEDICATION

To My Children,

David, Gina, Angela, and Aric

To My Nieces and Nephews,

Jason, Michael, Darren, Teresa, Kristi, Nicholas, Mark, Ryan,

May You Be Guided by the 7 Steps to Achieving Success.

I acknowledge that it is our God who has given me the talent and resources to share this book with my children and the rest of the world.

"If any of you lack wisdom, let him ask God, that giveth to all men liberally, and unbraided not: and it shall be given him."

Letter of James 1:5

ACKNOWLEDGEMENT

Patricia A. Sobotka

The completion of this book and workbooks would not be possible without the continuous support given by my wife, Patricia. Her ongoing, behind the scenes support of assisting in the delivery of the Achieving Life & Career Success seminar/workshops to countless individuals is truly appreciated.

TABLE OF CONTENTS

FOREWORD

Dr. Brian Harris
Founder & Chairman, the Partnering Group

I write this Foreword to this book with a lot of pride and joy. I have known Dennis Sobotka since 1990 and have admired his work in all the areas of his endeavors. Since that time he and I have travelled the world together as business partners and friends and I have come to regard him as a brother. I have crossed paths with many amazing people in my personal and business life but I have met no one with the combination of professional and personal qualities of Dennis. His consistent ability to balance the important dimensions of his life's journey, his business career, his charitable giving back and his family are exemplary. He can teach us all a lot about the secrets of "Achieving Life and Career Success". I am very pleased that he has decided to share his ideas and experiences through the writing of this book.

Elements of Success

The book provides a path for success and especially the blending of key elements required for success in life. We all strive for success but define it in different ways. It is an elusive term and in today's world of over-hyped celebrities it is easy to become confused, and even mislead, as to its real meaning. I have always believed that the way to better understand what success means lies in three areas. First is the choice of suitable role models whose accomplishments and qualities provide an inspiring example for us and help define a path to the goal of success for us. Second is the need to understand the elements that blend together to make up the true meaning of success. Success happens when we achieve goals for each element and accomplish the right balance among these elements as we go through life. And third is the willingness to do, as a mentor of mine once told me, a "brutal self-assessment" to uncover where your strengths and weaknesses are and to set goals that can systematically close the most important gaps in your capabilities and qualities. Dennis' book provides sound and practical guidance for addressing each of these three areas. It is a must read for anyone striving to develop and live a more balanced and successful life.

Importance of a Life Plan

Dennis has often called me his mentor. But as I've found out in my own journey, mentoring always goes both ways. The mentor learns just as much, if not more, from the mentee. This has certainly been the case in my 25 year relationship with Dennis. Let me illustrate this in a couple of ways. When I first met Dennis he was building a very successful career path with a highly respected supermarket retailer in upstate New York. I was asked by the company to bring in a new approach I had developed for how to manage a retailer's buying and merchandising functions. Dennis was appointed to be the project leader for my consulting work. At the time the new methods were becoming recognized by leading retailers around the world as the next generation of methods in these areas. Dennis confided in me that he had a ten year life plan and believed that part of his plan was to use his experience and knowledge to help other companies and their managers raise their performance and success levels. He asked me whether I would consider him joining with me to accomplish this goal of his. For the next 25 years that is what we have done together all around the world. But the lesson to share is that what gave him the guidance to make such a bold career move was the fact that he had a comprehensive and well thought out ten year plan as the path to success. Since then Dennis has shared two additional ten year plans with me and his decisions have been guided by these plans. Among the many valuable contributions of this book is that it provides us with a checklist of the key elements of a personal and professional ten year plan.

The Challenge of Balance

One of the biggest challenges we all face as we strive for success in our lives is how to achieve the right balance among our personal, family and professional endeavors. While there is no easy answer for most of us one of the secrets is to try to use similar approaches in each of these areas. If we have no synergy across these areas it is a lot more difficult to achieve a balance. Dennis has provided me and us with an excellent example of how to improve the likelihood of a successful balanced life. He has applied the methodology of his ten year planning approach to how he manages both his professional consulting career and even more impressively to how he has managed his charitable giving back and family activities. I remember how impressed I was when I learned about his "Achieving Life and Career Success" charity work especially the programs he conducted with young prison inmates who are preparing for life after their release. As expected, Dennis' methodology was to teach these young people how to develop a practical plan for their next phase of their lives. This was the same approach he used for his own career and life plan. By involving his wife Patricia and their children in his "Achieving Life and Career Success" seminar work he has also shown them, both by example and method, the value of developing and following a plan for life. As with any long lasting relationship, the boundary between mentor and mentee is a blurred one as the value of the mutual benefits becomes clear. Whether you strive to be a better mentor or mentee, Dennis' advice in this book gives us some important guidance for achieving success in this element of our lives.

Creating and Maintaining a Living Life Success Plan

While having a plan with its inherent goals is an obvious requirement for success whether it be within an organization or as an individual, it is not enough to ensure that these goals are accomplished. As we have seen many times during our consulting work, a plan achieves nothing if it "sits on the shelf" and if it is "a project that has to be completed". A good plan is a document that lives. It guides one's actions on a day-to-day basis. It is a living document. Its value is sustained because it is a source of continual learning. It provides a picture of what success looks like and what is required to get there. Several steps of Dennis' book provide important insights for what is needed to keep your plan connected to reality. Step 4 emphasizes the key role of being disciplined in the light of the many distractions we face as we move through life. It also highlights the importance of having gratitude for the gifts we have received. Good goals take shape through creative visualization, the ability to imagine what the accomplishment of a goal will look like and the path to achieving the goal. On a number of occasions over the years as Dennis and I have been challenged by especially difficult consulting assignments, it has been Dennis' ability to creatively visualize the outcome that has led us to the right recommendation. The practical insights into how to use this technique that are described in the book are a very valuable contribution to defining a path to success. Finally, true success is based on a lifetime of learning. This starts with the realization that the fastest way to expand one's level of knowledge is to realize how little we know. This inspires us to tap into the knowledge of others who have expertise in areas either directly related to our plan or areas that can extend our horizons in a synergistic way. These are the mentors and role models in our life. I have been amazed with the diversity of thinkers that Dennis has tapped into to expand his personal knowledge over the years. It has truly given him insights that are beyond the normal curve of expanded thinking. The book offers us advice as to how we can acquire new knowledge as we follow the "Odyssey of Learning" in our own lives.

A Practical Path for Success

"Achieving Life and Career Success" is a must read for anyone in search of a balanced and successful (in the true meaning of the word) life. It presents a unique blend of the attitudes, the disciplines, the creativity and the tools that are needed to achieve the true meaning and feeling of success. Dennis Sobotka is a living example of the power of these elements coming together. Reading his book will provide the methodology and the tools for incorporating these elements into a success plan for our lives. I have seen it work so well for Dennis, I have incorporated it into my life and I hope his words and example will inspire you to achieve an even higher level of success in your career and personal life. Enjoy the book.

Brian F. Harris Ph.D.

INTRODUCTION

Within Each Child is an Untold Success Story Yet to Unfold
~ Author Unknown

Our Mission

It is our commitment and passion to provide individuals with the **spark**, the **vision**, the **path**, and the **tools** needed to achieve their full potential for success.

You have just taken the first step to success by investing your time and money into reading this workbook. The intent of this workbook is to provide direction to all people who are seeking self-improvement and have a desire to achieve life and career success. The magic of this workbook is the *7 Step Process* that delivers a specific step-by-step method to create your own customized written life success plan. This personalized life success plan is unique and powerful with results that have delivered significant changes in the lives of others.

This 7 Step Process for achieving life and career success can be used effectively with a wide-range of individuals. It is designed to help the non-professional and professional person on their path to success. The emphasis is on individual dreams to success which is why our 7 Step Process is effective with all ages, groups and organizations. Our process has been used by companies with middle and senior management, advanced professionals in their fields of studies, public school and college students, along with community groups and organizations.

Let us summarize what will be covered in each of the 7 steps to give clarity of this process.

Step 1 - Defining Success: You will establish your individualized definition of success by reflecting on your personal dreams and desires. This will be facilitated by challenging you to think bigger than your present self-imposed limitations.

Step 2 - Your Path of Life: "Where Have You Been?" This is an analytic review of your past life activities in which you will identify your strengths and weaknesses. These learnings will help to build your future path of life to achieve your dreams of success.

Step 3 - Your Ten Year Goals: "Where Are You Going?" A combination of long term and short term goals are needed to achieve your definition of success. First, you will identify long term goals which will be incorporated into a ten year plan. Then you will establish short term goals directed towards accomplishing your long term goals in your ten year plan. Milestones of accomplishments will be identified along your path towards success.

Step 4 - Attitudes and Disciplines: The theme of this section is to provide you with daily success tools and the required changes needed when using them.

Step 5 - Creative Visualization: This is the most powerful daily success tool that can be used to achieve your short and long term goals which will lead to your dreams of success.

Step 6 - Cloud of Unknowing: "You Don't Know What You Don't Know." This part of the process recognizes voids of knowledge. Mentors and role models will be identified in this step that will assist you in filling these voids of knowledge.

Step 7 - Odyssey of Learning: Personal development is emphasized in this step to encourage your continued improvement in skills that will assist you in completing your short and long term goals.

We will introduce the concept called the odyssey of learning in which you will reach out to unique individuals for additional learnings.

The teachings in this workbook are written in conjunction with our seminar/workshops. Our success seminar called "Achieving Life and Career Success" is a hands-on, personalized approach for individuals to explore their inner dreams and then manifest them into reality. The same 7 Step Process presented provides an individualized written life success plan that is found in all three of our products; the book, a workbook and at the seminars. Individuals from different countries and walks of life have attended our success seminars and completed their written life success plans over the past 20 years.

The teaching approach used consists of three parts both in this workbook and during our success seminars. These three parts are:
1. Teaching the core learnings.
2. Completing the exercise worksheets based on the core learnings.
3. Summarizing the workshops and engaging in open discussions, affording the opportunity for individual and group participation.

This workbook contains the first two parts, teaching the core learnings and completing the exercises. The third part, open discussions, can be achieved when sharing your learnings from the workbook with other family members and friends. The benefits of sharing with others is the positive reinforcement that will strengthen your desired success, along with you becoming a catalyst for them to develop their own success path. A word of caution, when sharing your exercises with others, do not allow negative attitude from other individuals to influence your personal dreams and aspirations.

One of the challenges faced as a facilitator is motivating individuals to think "bigger" with their dreams and aspirations. Too many of us have self-imposed limitations that create barriers to achieving our goals and ambitions. You justify in your minds and hearts why you cannot dream for something larger than what is the norm or expected results. This is one of your greatest challenges to success. After reading this workbook you will be among the believers and achievers.

Upon finishing this workbook and its exercises, you will have completed a written and individualized life success plan by following the 7 Step process. This should be considered an event to celebrate and what better way than by sharing your written life success plan with other positive people. By declaring and sharing your goals and plans, you are reinforcing your conscious and subconscious mind towards reaching your dreams of success. If you feel comfortable, please email me your success stories so that we can celebrate your achievements as well.

So let's get started on this journey together.

STEP 1

Define Success

"What is your Definition of Success?"

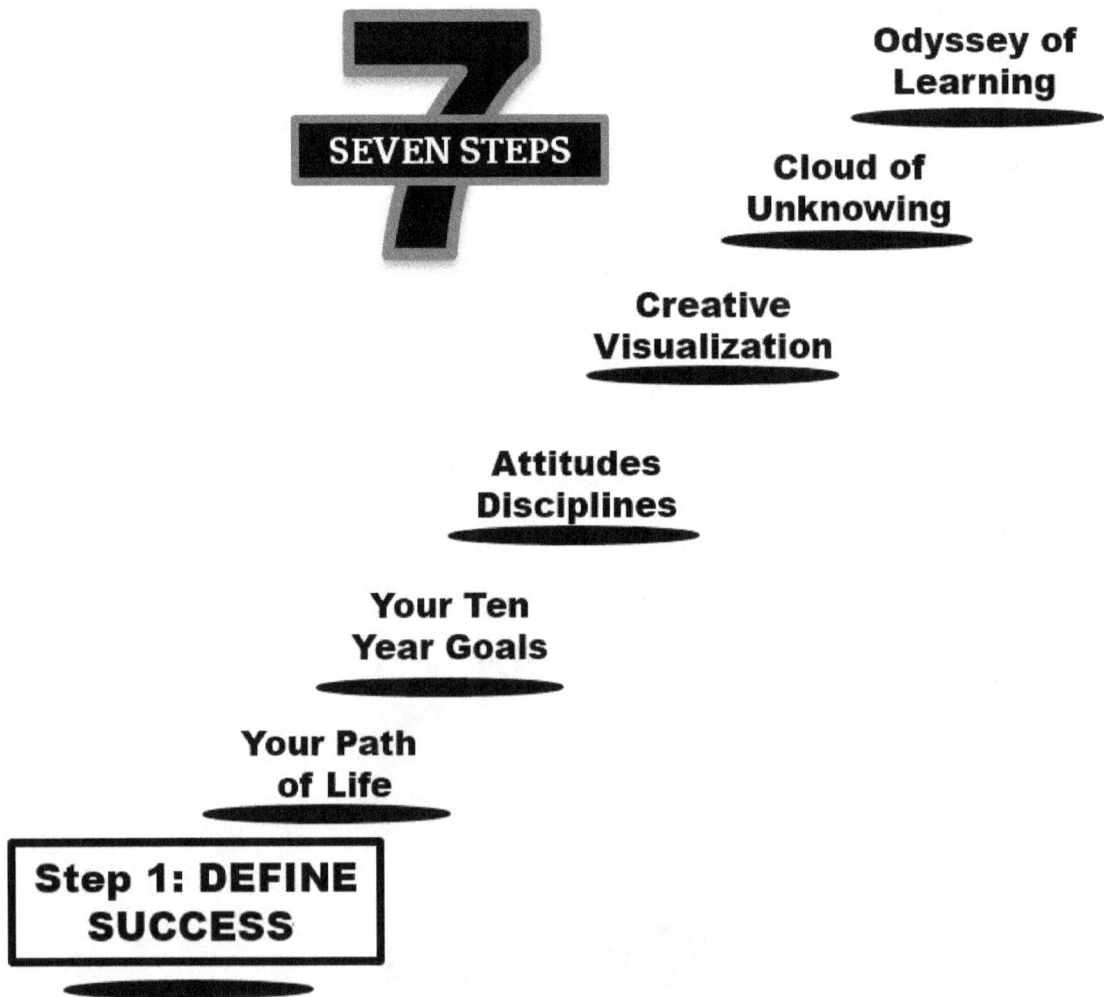

7 SEVEN STEPS

- Odyssey of Learning
- Cloud of Unknowing
- Creative Visualization
- Attitudes Disciplines
- Your Ten Year Goals
- Your Path of Life
- **Step 1: DEFINE SUCCESS**

God doesn't require us to succeed; He only requires that we try.
~ Mother Teresa, Albanian–born Indian Roman Catholic Nun

Have you ever really asked yourself this question, "What does success mean to me?" Too many people go through life measuring their success without ever really asking themselves what success means to them. Why is that? Is it because you base it on what society rates as success; such as wealth or fame or your career? Or are you just numbed by all your responsibilities in life that you never take time to reflect on what you think success means to you. Many of you will be waiting for this workbook to provide you with a definition of success for you to work with. This workbook and teaching process does not give you a predetermined definition of success. Rather it facilitates your quantifying and defining what is really important to you in life, which will be your individualized definition of success. This is one of the many reasons which makes this workbook different and special.

"What does success mean to you?" As you ponder this, you will find that your definition of success will be unique to your desires, dreams and goals in life. After all, why should my success be measured by another? The Merriam Webster Dictionary defines the word success as: 1. *favorable or desired outcome; 2. the gaining of wealth or fame; 3. one that succeeds.* Upon completion of this step, you will define and better understand your definition of success.

Assuming you are reading this workbook because you feel that spark of desire to achieve life and career success, the plan is to jump start that spark and provide you with the tools needed to prepare your path to success. This workbook is the stimulant to get you in motion and is designed to outline all the steps needed throughout your path to success. It will open your mind to new visions of your dreams and will help you recognize barriers and distractions that could present obstacles along the way. You will learn techniques in dealing with these obstacles and methods to identify your inner-strengths that will overcome these challenges.

Success does not come easy. This workbook is designed to provide you with tools and practices that will make your quest for success easy and attainable. The exercises in this workbook will teach you to establish goals and objectives that will be the foundation for your individual path for success. This workbook is not a read-only reference, it is an interactive approach that provides you with action steps and applications to your daily lifestyle. Be prepared to think differently and adapt new ways of dealing with everyday activities. The difference between this success process and others is the exercises in this workbook provide you with new found learnings about yourself that you can apply to your everyday life. You will identify areas of weaknesses and strengths that will then be applied to new daily habits and attitudes that will move you closer to being successful.

As you embark on this path of achieving life and career success, it is my belief that this workbook will prepare you in all ways to succeed in this quest. It will prove to be a motivator for some and possibly a life changer for others. My hope is that you will embrace the tools you learn and implement the techniques and methods resulting from your new learnings. Let's get started.

One Life to Live

As indicated in the introduction of this workbook, references will be made to the Success Seminars I present that are designed with the same format as this workbook.

In our Success seminars, I open the presentation by asking the audience this question, "Everyone is given exactly the same thing... What is that?" As expected, there are many different answers and perspectives from those in attendance, but the common answer is "One Life." You are all given exactly the same thing, "One Life!" Everyone seems to agree with this commonality. That leads to the second question "How are you going to use your One Life?" The answer seems simple enough, "It is Your Choice!"

You have the freedom to choose how you decide to live your life. Make the choice now to improve your skills and follow the process outlined in this workbook that will help you map out your personalized path to success. How will you decide to live your life? What decisions will you make that will generate changes in your life that will equate into success for you? It is both your choice and your free will to make these decisions and changes.

Success requires change! Yet, so many people truly struggle to believe they can effect change in their lives. How many of you are really comfortable in making changes in your life? For those of you who will embrace the learnings in this workbook, be prepared to accept the challenge of change. If you implement all the learnings, you may find yourself faced with more than just minor changes in your life, you may experience a personal transformation. This will occur through adjustments and adaptions to new disciplines, habits and attitudes. After all, success requires change and change produces new results. Do not be afraid of transforming yourself into that individual who can make their dreams become their reality. What transformation do you need to make that will produce the results of a successful life?

You have but one life to live, how you choose to live it is your choice.
~ Dennis J Sobotka, Author, Mentor & Business Consultant

Transformation to Success

Transforming oneself requires a different mindset that will open your path to success. You need to embrace change so that you can incorporate new learnings into your daily lifestyle. View your misfortunes as growth experiences to learn from and ignore these distractions that can lead you astray. You need to stay focused on your objectives and most importantly, adopt a positive attitude that will overcome your daily trials and keep you steadfast on the path to success.

If you were questioning your ability to transform your life into one of success because of your socioeconomic status, or your parents failures, or adversities that you had to deal with in your life, then you need to be introduced to successful people who never allowed those barriers to stop them from reaching their success.

For instance, did you know that Oprah Winfrey had to overcome much hardship and childhood adversity before becoming one of the most successful and richest people in the world today? Oprah is no stranger to poverty, parental neglect, and even sexual abuse as a child. She ran away from home at age fourteen to flee from her abusers. Yet despite all the odds against her, Oprah reached success in her personal and professional life and became the first female African-American billionaire. What a transformation.

What about physical challenges, are they enough to warrant settling for less than what your dreams are? Not if your name is Bethany Hamilton. Bethany was an avid surfer and a normal 13 year-old until an almost deadly shark attack resulted in her losing her left arm. Rather than wallowing in pity, Bethany returned to surfing within a month after the attack. Two years later she won first place in the Explorer Women's Division of the NSSA National Championships. Bethany was a champion despite her challenges. She never gave up on her dream.

Stephen King's books are read globally, yet if I told you that his first book was rejected 30 times and he threw it in the trash, would you believe it? Well it's true. If it weren't for his wife who retrieved it from the garbage and urged him to continue to pursue his dreams, he would have never sold 350 million copies of his multiple books to date, nor would his books have been made into countless major motion pictures. He had a vision and he stuck with it.

Benjamin Franklin dropped out of school at a young age because his parents couldn't afford to keep him in school. That didn't stop him from becoming the great man he was, instead he overcame his adversities and taught himself through avid reading and experiences as an apprentice in the newspaper business. He became a great inventor and one of America's Founding Fathers.

Another successful man you read about in our history books is Thomas Edison, who is credited with inventing the lightbulb. However, Edison is said to have failed more than 1,000 to 10,000 times while attempting to invent the lightbulb. I imagine that after the one-hundredth failure, it would have been reasonable for anyone to give up that dream. But rather than giving up, Edison chose to remain positive about his vision and was quoted saying, ""I have not failed. I've just found 10,000 ways that won't work." Thomas Edison never gave up on his dream.

Would you believe me if I told you that a very famous and accomplished producer was rejected twice from University of Southern California when applying into their film school? Steven Spielberg, the world famous producer best known for his work of "Shindler's List," "Jaws," "E.T." and "Jurassic Park" was rejected. Now look at his range of successes.

There are so many other great success stories that are riddled with overcoming adversities, Nelson Mandela, Franklin Roosevelt, Richard Branson, Vincent Van Gogh, Stephen Hawking, etc. You understand the point here, despite your adversities, you can achieve life and career success if you are determined to do so. Don't let challenges change your direction, rather use them as stepping stones and remain on course.

Often we are ignorant to the stories behind well-known successful people, not realizing they have overcome similar adversities as we face. The intent of introducing them in this step was to convince you that it is possible for you to experience success no matter where you are in your life, no matter what barriers you face, or what limitations you feel have been placed upon you. This is the most important concept for you to grasp in order for you to realize that "the sky's the limit" that your dreams of success are within your reach.

People are always blaming their circumstances for what they are. I don't believe in circumstances. The people who get on in the world are the people who get up and look for the circumstances they want, and if they can't find them, make them.
~ George Bernard Shaw, Nobel-Prize-Winning Irish Playwright

Success Is All Around Us

There are many success stories you hear about every day in the media. Donald Trump has his hotels and buildings with all the glitter and glamour that goes along with being Donald Trump. Bill Gates has become one of the richest men in America based upon the computer age. Warren Buffet is one of the wealthiest, most successful stock investors in the world. Michael Jordan is one of the greatest basketball players of all times. He holds approximately 200 Basketball records and today is a very successful businessman. Barrack Obama is the first black president of the world's richest country. These are some of the superstars of success!

Look at other successful individuals like Mother Teresa. There's no flash, no glitz she gave her entire life to helping people. She reached out and touched those who needed help. She received nothing monetary in return, yet Mother Teresa achieved her definition of success.

   www.achievingsuccesscenter.com

It's obvious that Mother Teresa's definition of success was much different than that of Donald Trump's or President Obama's and probably even different from yours. What is your definition of success?

These are just a sprinkling of the most famous showcases of success. Where did they come from? The same place as you and I. What sets them apart? They no doubt had their own definitions of success and they followed well-chosen paths to their dreams. I hope that sharing the success of others, both those who overcame adversities to reach success and those who aspired to greatness, has convinced you that you can define your own success story and make it happen.

The future belongs to those who believe in the beauty of their dreams.
~ Eleanor Roosevelt, First Lady of the United States

Defining Your Success

Success comes from having dreams and realizing those dreams. Within each of us there is the potential to realize our dreams, in fact, everyone should have their own idea of what success means to them. Yet, so many of us fail to put our dreams into action. You learned that transforming your dreams into physical reality requires a positive attitude, focus on objectives, and embracing new learnings.

How do you do this? You start by visualizing what you want for your success. Then you begin to take action.

The Four Important Elements related to Success

Although there are many factors that influence a person's success in life, there are four important elements crucial in understanding and embracing success. These four elements are the following;

1. Dream Big
2. Believe in Yourself
3. Embrace a Positive Attitude
4. Visualize Your Success

Knowing there are multiple factors that will influence your success over your lifetime is generally understood by everyone. These factors will differ from one person to another. However there are universal tools that can be used regardless of one's situation that will have a strong impact on the outcome of your success in life. It is my intent in this book to provide you with exercises/tools you can implement as they relate to your individual situation.

Let's begin by understanding the impact of these four elements on your path to success.

1. **Dream big**, or better said, "Reach for the stars." Do not place limitations on your dreams but rather make a conscious decision to dream much bigger than you are imagining today. Then use the tools in this book to make those dreams a reality. Don't settle for something that is less than what you desire. Rather, reflect on what would be the ideal life you want. What are all of your needs that would translate into a lifetime of success? You will be asked in the first exercise, found in this step, to write in as much detail your dreams definition of success so that you can use this to realize your own dreams. Research indicates that when you share your goals and aspirations with friends and family, it improves your chances of reaching them by reinforcing your conscious and subconscious mind.

In a research study by Dominican University of California, psychology professor Dr. Gail Matthews included the results in a 2013 Forbes article, which were "that writing down your goals, sharing them with friends, and sending your friends regular updates about your progress can boost your chances of succeeding. The study showed that people who merely thought about their goals and how to reach them succeeded less than 50% of the time, while people who wrote goals down, and enlisted friends to help them by sending regular progress reports succeeded closer to 75% of the time." Thus we believe that the more you discuss your dreams and goals, the more likely you will achieve them.

To encourage you to dream bigger than what you may be dreaming now, let me share with you a story I refer to as "Five Little Fingers/Five Big Goals." The purpose of this story is to illustrate dreaming big, regardless of your age or your current level of success. The story is centered on a family member of a participant at one of my seminars. All of the same exercises included in this book, along with a number of additional ones, are presented at my seminars. At the completion of the seminars, I encourage the participants to share their results from their workshops with their families.

The day after the seminar, Edith, one of the participants, offered to share her daughter's response to the dreams and goal setting workshop at a meeting with other managers who also had attended the seminar. Andrea, Edith's young five-year-old daughter, told her mother that she had five goals. As Edith shared these goals, the adults in the room, including myself, were simply amazed at how big her goal setting was in relationship to her young age of five.

"Andrea's Five Little Fingers / Five Big Goals"

1. To learn how to cook!
2. To have her own TV cooking show!
3. To travel and see Paris!
4. To have $1,000,000 pesos.
5. To learn to play music!

The lesson learned from this young child is that she challenged herself beyond her age, which is one of the key components in dreaming big. This five-year-old girl listed goals that were proportionately bigger than many of the goals set by those in attendance. Andrea and her five big goals were the perfect motivating factor to push the attendees to believe in significantly bigger goals for themselves. I include this example to encourage you to break the paradigm you may have when it comes to dreaming big and to reinforce setting goals that reach beyond your comfort zone.

Another example of dreaming big is the heroism of Martin Luther King Jr. When Martin Luther King Jr. said, "I have a dream," it wasn't just some utopian rhetoric he was spouting. He worked diligently and passionately to fulfill his dream. He helped to form the Southern Christian Leadership Conference and was named its first president. He wrote and published books, and he continually spoke out on civil-rights issues and social change. In a typical year of peaceful demonstrations, Dr. King traveled 780,000 miles and made 208 speeches. He became a role model for countless African Americans who adopted his dream, among them Maya Angelou. Through it all, he faced huge obstacles to his dream. King lived and died for his dream of freedom for all people, and there is still a lot of work to be done to fulfill his dream. The fact is Dr. King accomplished his dream of helping African Americans to individually and collectively raise the awareness of equality for all people.

Reach high, for stars lie hidden in your soul. Dream deep, for every dream precedes the goal.
~ Pamela Vaull Starr, Poet, Artist, & Writer

2. **Believe in yourself**, or better said, "Remove all predetermined and self-imposed limitations." You are not defined by where you live, nor by your cultural upbringing, nor by your parents, but rather you can decide who you want to be. The key step is to remove self-imposed limitations. The definition of self-imposed is "something that you require or expect of yourself, rather than something required by another". The definition of limitations is "a restriction or a defect, or the act of imposing restrictions". Therefore, based on these definitions, it is within your control to decide what you expect of yourself and to release all restrictions from your dreams and goals.

The life you lead will be determined by the choices you make in life. You can decide who you want to be and how you will go about aspiring to be that person regardless of your socioeconomic status, or your cultural upbringing, or your physical make-up, etc. You are not defined by your parent's successes or failures. You are not defined by your wealth or your social class. You are not defined by your location. It is your inner-self that will give you the strength to make conscious decisions that will influence your success in life.

I have always been fascinated by elephants and while reading about their life in captivity I came across information that was the epitome of self-imposed limitations. As a learning example, I would like to share the following story about baby elephants.

When baby elephants come into the world of captivity, one of the first things they encounter is having a metal shackle secured around their ankles and then chained into cement to prevent them from moving beyond the limited space of their cage. This is standard practice to break the spirit of this wild animal. Why? Because when the elephant grows to be full size, no shackle will be able to withstand their strength as they instinctively try to break through their captivity. Therefore, while the animal is still young enough, the baby elephant is too small to break the chain. They will try continuously over weeks to break the chain and fail. At a certain point in time the baby elephant concedes that they can never break that shackle and chain that holds them in place.

Thus when the elephant grows to full size and has the power to break that shackle, they are not tempted to do so based on what they have learned in the past. The elephants "mindset and belief" is that the chain can never be broken, thus the elephant stops trying to break it. In reality, the elephant could break the chain with very little effort.

People are just like the baby elephant as they accept and adopt mindsets and beliefs filled with many limitations to what they can and cannot do in life. Many of these self-imposed beliefs come from good intentions, such as parents who do not want their children to experience failure and therefore hold them back, or extended family members downgrading others in the family unit, breeding self-imposed restrictions. Teachers who use grades to rate students without offering the positive encouragement to strive for better. There will be many people in your life suppressing your dreams rather than reinforcing your spirit of success. As a society, we tend to sensationalize all the negative which leads to deflating the spirit of the majority and their zeal to excel and succeed. Too often we inflict our own self-imposed restrictions.

This element of believing in yourself translates into a strong, self-confident individual possessing high self-esteem. This is achieved through believing in oneself by trying experiences despite adversities and without fear of failure knowing you can accomplish many of them. This is best reflected in a quote by Michael Jordan when he states, *"I've missed more than 9000 shots in my career. I've lost almost 300 games. 26 times, I have been trusted to take the game winning shot and missed. I have failed over and over again in my life. And that is why I succeed."*

I would like to conclude this section with these last thoughts, expel the idea of blaming others for not reaching your full potential or achieving your dreams. This only sabotages your ability to believe in yourself.

Change your mindset to that of positive thinking and overcoming your self-imposed limitations. Self-imposed limitations of your dreams is like a disease and your challenge is to remove yourself from those who harbor this disease.

Your success depends mainly upon what you think of yourself and whether you believe in yourself.
~ William J. H. Boetcker, Religious Leader & Public Speaker

3. **Embrace a positive attitude**, or better said, "Being positive doesn't cost you anything, but it buys a lot." What does it cost you to wake each morning with the attitude you will face life with positivity and promise? When you strive to be positive about all aspects of your life, regardless of the cards you are dealt, you can make anything happen. It is like that new car you just bought, you never noticed others driving them until you purchased one for yourself. Then your mind is drawn to all those same model cars on the road. The same principle applies to being positive. Your attitude will be noticed by all the other positive thinking people who will be drawn to you. The more positive thinking, the more effective you will be in reaching your success. In Step 4, you will find exercises to help you be more equipped in starting each day with the right attitude. You will be reminded to stop blaming others for your failures, as it is easy to justify your shortcomings if you can switch the blame. Changing your "mindset" is an important step to overcoming negativism and resetting yourself to being a positive thinker.

Human beings, by changing the inner attitudes of their minds,
can change the outer aspects of their lives
~ William James, US Philosopher & Psychologist

4. **Visualize your success**, or better said, "Seeing is believing." Visualize what you want in your life and how you plan on achieving it. Through repetitive visualization, and with every detail rehearsed, you can program your path to success. You will move closer to reaching your goals and following your plan to success when you can visualize yourself in action. Step 5 is dedicated to the power of creative visualization and you will learn in that step how to use this invaluable technique in your path to success. You will be enlightened by other successful people who have used visualization and credit much of their success to creative visualization. This powerful tool is so underutilized because it is not taught in traditional schools. While reading Step 5, open your mind to embracing creative visualization and incorporating it into your daily activities. If you do so, you will find yourself among the many who have credited this technique to their success in life.

Vision is the art of seeing what is invisible to others.
~Jonathan Swift, essayist, poet & cleric

The Magic of Visualization

The magic of achieving success requires your ability to visualize your success along with physically working towards reaching it. At times, your visualization can be stronger in effecting success than your physical commitments. Now, do not get me wrong, physical work and commitment to accomplish anything is necessary. However, studies have indicated that mental practices can be at times as effective in manifesting change.

Srinivasan Pillay, the CEO of NeuroBusiness Group and award-winning author, wrote about visualization and it's manifestation into physical action in the following article, "The Science of Visualization: Maximizing Your Brain's Potential during the Recession," excerpted from the Huffpost Healthy Living issue on November 17, 2011.

"Although visualization was regarded as 'new age hype' for many years, research has shown that there is a strong scientific basis for how and why visualization works. It is now a well-known fact that we stimulate the same brain regions when we visualize an action and when we actually perform that same action. For example, when you visualize lifting your right hand, it stimulates the same part of the brain that is activated when you actually lift your right hand. This shared area of brain activation when we imagine an action and perform it has been demonstrated extensively in the scientific literature . . . In fact, athletes have known about this power for a long time. Expert athletes use imagery and visualization to run their races in their goal times. Studies have shown that these athletes first imagine running the race in the goal time in as much detail as possible and are then able to execute it after practicing visualizing this. One study showed that '. . . visualizations under hypnosis enabled nationally ranked Stanford male gymnasts to execute for the first time several complex tricks that they had been working on for over a year. These gymnasts were able to eliminate timing errors in the tricks, to increase flexibility, and, possibly, to concentrate strength . . .' Another study showed that youth soccer players increased their confidence in playing when they visualized their moves. Visualization has also been shown to improve high jumpers clearing the bar."

What people need to realize is the percentage of time and focus given to mental visualization versus physical work determines the speed and ability for your dreams to become your success. Most people give 100% or 99% to the physical and zero or 1% to the visual. This is wrong! The percentage for visualization should be increased to at least 5% to start with, and then a continued progression upward.

Your mind is like the "computer" and your visualization and hand written goals are like the "software". You need the software installed to run the computer. The more detail and time you give to the "software," the more your mind and body will work together towards unconsciously and subconsciously fulfilling your dreams of success.

Excerpted from Creative Visualization by Shakti Gawain. "Creative visualization is the technique of using your imagination to create what you want in your life. There is nothing at all new, strange, or unusual about creative visualization. You are already using it every day -- every minute in fact. It is your natural power of imagination, the basic creative energy of the universe, which you use constantly, whether or not you are aware of it . . . In creative visualization you use your imagination to create a clear image, idea, or feeling of something you wish to manifest. Then you continue to focus on the idea, feeling, or picture regularly, giving it positive energy until it becomes objective reality . . . in other words, until you actually achieve what you have been imagining."

Your software of visualization that you program into your mind (computer) is the most important learning in this book and in our seminar/workshops. It can have a positive impact on your life, your family's life, and those you love. Visualization is the magic to your success.

Dennis' Personal Story Defining Success

In reality, we all have our own measure of what success means to us. And even then, the ingredients will vary from time to time as our personal values change. My definition of success has changed over the years due in part to how I was raised and to my own personal growth. The following story illustrates how my father's early death affected me in terms of what I visualized about my future success at a fairly young age.

My father died when I was 6 years old, at which point my mother, two sisters and I moved into my grandmother's house (my grandfather died a year later). As a boy growing up, I watched my mother and grandmother try their best to keep our household together. They both worked in the school system, one as a janitor and the other as a cook's helper. They didn't make much money, but enough to maintain the house and to feed, clothe and provide for the family.

To afford a vacation we always drove the station wagon, since flying was out of the question. My mother sewed all of our costumes for Halloween and parties and most of our school outfits as well. We had a large field where vegetables were grown, and my mother and grandmother spent many arduous hours canning everything imaginable from the garden. I vividly recall the large pantry off the kitchen with its stacks and stacks of canned goods. In retrospect, I realize how lucky we children were to have such resourceful and loving providers.

It was back then that I began to visualize my dream about someday being financially secure and independent. For a while, my only definition of success was financial success.

However, as you mature, you will find your priorities shift which means your definition of success may change as well. For me, what once revolved around money, transformed to include having a loving relationship of a close-knit family. This was a significant transformation considering the family dynamics I grew up in. There is one personal memory that holds very strong in my mind: I could not tell my mother I loved her until I was twenty years old. I don't begrudge myself this fact, it's just that showing emotion in our family wasn't a part of our early development training. Today, with my own family, expressing our unconditional love for one another is one of the most important things we do. I know if we had to, we could survive without a lot of money and much of what we own, but we could not survive without sharing our love in a multitude of ways. This reflects my definition of success adjusting with time and maturity, an emotional transformation.

This summarizes the four important elements for your path to success.

1. Dream Big
2. Believe in Yourself
3. Embrace a Positive Attitude
4. Visualize Your Success

It is the purpose of this book to offer you tools to define your success and map out your path to reach your full potential. Each exercise will build upon the previous one, all with the intent of developing your personalized written life success plan.

If you paint in your mind a picture of bright and happy expectations,
you put yourself into a condition conducive to your goal.
~ Norman Vincent Peale, Minister & Author

Exercises

What follows is the first in a series of exercises in this workbook. They are similar to the workshops we ask participants to complete in our seminars. These exercises will be most valuable if you write down your answers and also adjust them as you learn more about the process and yourself. In each exercise, record as much detail as you can to capture your life success plan. If you have any difficulty doing a particular exercise, come back to it after you have read more of this workbook. In fact, we encourage you to take a second, and third pass to each exercise. After you complete the exercises, you will have completed your own personalized success workbook for your life and career plan. We will be using a broad base of examples to help meet the various needs of all our readers.

This is an example of our personalized "Life Success Plan" booklet.

TAKEAWAYS: Your Dreams of Success

- Definition of Success, your dreams, is unique to each person.

- Your personal definition of success is within your dreams.

- You can have success in your life if you decide you want it and you make good choices.

- Accept change to allow for personal transformation toward success.

- Writing down your dreams is the first step towards achieving success.

- The more detailed your dreams of success, the more likely you will achieve it.

Exercise #1: Your Dreams of Success

Objective:

- To capture your personal definition of success by asking yourself to reach into your dreams and write down the details.

Steps:

- Close your eyes, block everything else out for three to five minutes, and think about your dreams of success.

- Remember to dream big, no self-imposed limitations.

- Put in writing, in as much detail as possible, what your dreams of success are as you have just visualized them.

- After you have written down your dreams of success, you can revisit it to make refinements as there are no right or wrong definitions of success. The objective is to capture what success means to you.

Achieving Success

EXAMPLE: Your Dreams / Your Definition of Success

My dream is to get into Miami of Ohio College and earn a degree in computer programming. I plan on getting a scholarship so that I can afford to go there in my freshman year. I dream of completing college with high honors so that I will be marketable with a bachelor in science degree, majoring in computer science.

While living away at college, I dream of meeting a wonderfully supportive, loving, and giving person who will share their life with me. We will get married in my hometown and settle there to raise our family. We will have three children, all healthy and happy.

I plan on setting up my own computer tech company, which will someday go public and provide me with financial security and independence. My company will be worth billions and I will employee thousands of people. My name will be known by all for pioneering new technology.

Traveling will be important for family vacations. We will travel some place different each year, expanding our experiences globally. I want to travel the Mediterranean, each year visiting a different country including Spain, France, Italy, Greece and then travel through Asia.

My cars will range from family vehicles to classic automobiles. My signature car will be a 1969 retrofitted mustang convertible, canary yellow with black interior.

After living in a two story home while building my business, our family will eventually move to Scottsdale, Arizona, in an estate home that has an enclosed pool that I can swim laps in everyday.

I can see myself an old man of 100 years of age, still healthy and traveling the world.

Your Dreams / Your Definition of Success

Your Dreams of Success

Career

Travel

Money

Family

Directions: Record your dreams or aspirations of what you consider to bring success in life. This is very individualized.

STEP 2

Your Path of Life
"Where Have You Been?"

7 SEVEN STEPS

Odyssey of Learning

Cloud of Unknowing

Creative Visualization

Attitudes Disciplines

Your Ten Year Goals

Step 2: YOUR PATH OF LIFE

Define Success

The elevator to success is out of order.
You'll have to use the stairs... one step at a time.
~Joe Girard, Author & Salesman

Where Have You Been Leads To Where Are You Going.

Once you have your personal definition of success in writing, it becomes interesting to look at your life from two different points of view: *Where you have been* and *where you are going*. In other words, you can look at how you have lived your life in the past (your life history) and how you will live your life in the future (your future goals). However, before you take a look at your future, it is wise to look at how you have chosen to live your life up until now. You need to learn from your past successes and failures but understand these will not define your future success. In this step, you will focus on the "where have you been" and first define the highs and lows of your past experiences. It will not be until Step 3 that you will focus on "where you are going" by defining your goals and your future path. We will also introduce later in this step a strategy of examining your strengths, weaknesses, opportunities and threats, which is referred to as your SWOT.

Think about what you have experienced in your life so far, and who or what helped shape those experiences. What have you learned from your past? A great part of what you have experienced is a result of decisions you've already made. Through this process of examining your past you will develop better self-awareness and self-understanding. This process will identify your strengths, weaknesses, opportunities and threats you have developed in your life.

Unfortunately, there are no high school or college courses that teach the concept of how to reflect and learn from your past path of life. To do this, we will discuss the many elements that build your path of life and help you document the learnings that come from it. Let's take a look at the different paths.

The Various Paths of Life

Your life's path begins the day you are born—when you are utterly dependent on the outside factors. These factors may include an abundance of love or a lack of love, a wealth of learning or an insufficient means of guidance, a nurturing environment or a broken home life. The support you receive during your developmental years influences the initial shape of your life's path. Without even knowing or understanding it, you may have faced challenges in your formative years. However those challenges do not need to shape your current path, as it is never too late to make the necessary changes in your life.

If you were to refer to the examples in the chart below, you will see different paths of life. Many of us will climb the ladder of success for a while, hit a plateau, regroup, and then continue to the next plateau. Or you may experience a number of peaks (highs) and valleys (lows), but not necessarily any straight lines to the top. Eventually you may reach your peak of success, but it may take more time and effort to get there than you envisioned. Rarely does it happen overnight.

Some people's lives seem blessed—they start out at the bottom and, like a rocket, they shoot straight up to their pinnacles of success. What a feat! Unfortunately this does not apply to most of us. Some paths of life might look like the following. Do any of them resemble yours?

Different Paths of Life

SWEET PATH

UP & DOWN PATH

CHALLENGING PATH

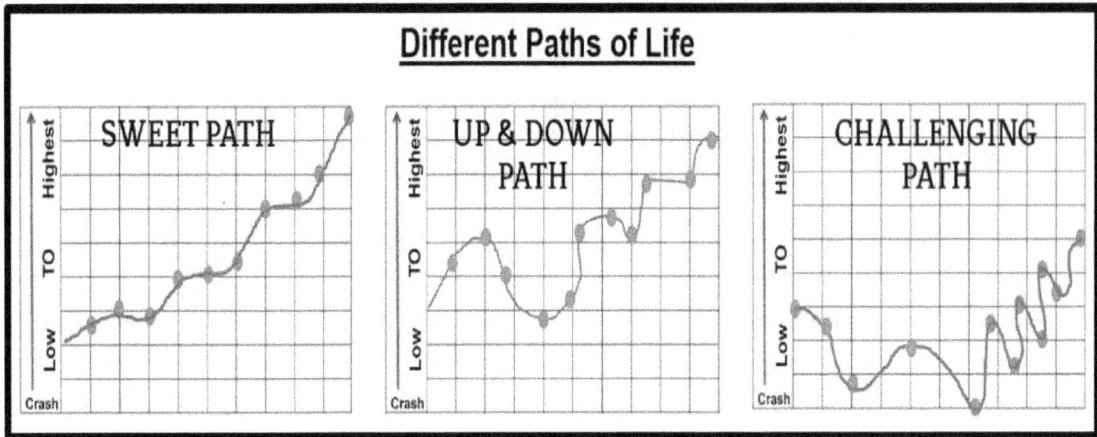

Your path in life will take on many forms, rarely remaining steady. It becomes a challenge just trying to balance between our careers and personal life. How many of us vacillate between too much emphasis on careers or an overly abundance of social activities, never really living a balanced life? This imbalance can lead to abuses in either direction. Being referred to as a workaholic suggests there is a neglect of your personal life, whereas indulging in excessive pleasures questions your commitment to your career. Neither equates to success, rather an extreme in either direction creates imbalances that could foster challenges with family dysfunction, work failures, consequences of drugs and alcohol abuse, pregnancy, or reckless driving. Everyone's life history is unique and we will help you identify your SWOT from your life history later in this step.

This next section will help identify five elements that are key to understanding your path in life.

Path of Life's Highs and Lows

The Path of Life takes many forms but is generally a series of highs and lows, hopefully with an abundance of highs and plateaus that are the base for your next series of upward swings. The following diagram highlights the five elements in the cycles of life, they are; upswings/highs, plateaus, low/dips, stop points and crash & burn.

Your Path of Life: Identify your
HIGHS & LOWS in Your Life Cycle

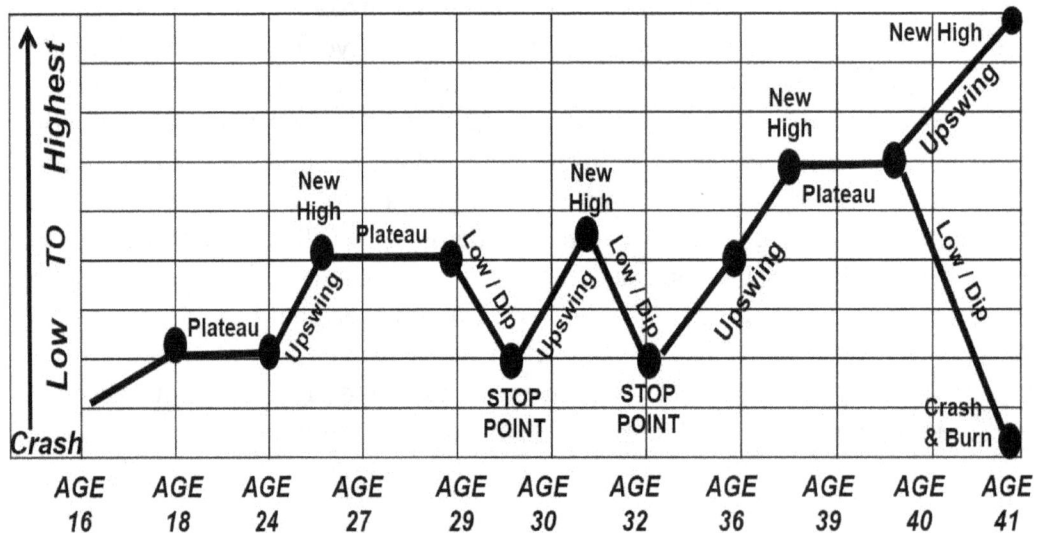

Elements of a Path of Life

Have you ever felt on top of the world, when you think you have control and balance in your life? That's a great feeling. Then one day, your timing is off, or you make a poor decision, or you're in the wrong place at the wrong time, and now this changes everything. You went from feeling on top of the world, to a new low. Maybe it's bad enough that you *think* you've hit rock bottom. It can be as simple as saying something inappropriate to your boss or as devastating as making the wrong turn which results in a motor vehicle accident. Whichever the scenario, you get a feeling in your stomach that you've really screwed up. This happens to everyone. We all inevitably experience low points in our journey.

The important thing is to recognize when it's happening to you, and to take note of how you react to the highs and lows. It's equally important to learn from your experiences. Let's take a look at these five key elements to the cycles of life which are outlined below.

1. **HIGH/UPSWINGS.** You will experience highs/upswings when you accomplish the right balance in your life. This occurs when you have reached specific goals, achieved work-family balance, something special happens to you, or other victories that occur in your life. Stop to enjoy and celebrate these highs. Recognize why and how these highs have been achieved to repeat them as often as possible. Later in the book we will discuss disciplines and attitudes that will help sustain the highs for longer periods of time for maximum benefit.

2. **PLATEAUS.** Once you have reached a high or achieved a goal, you may find yourself at a plateau. A plateau exists while you work towards another high in your life. It is during this plateau that you gain more experience, reexamine your next goals, or re-energize. The point is, from this plateau your next upswing will eventually start.

3. **LOW/DIPS.** Lows will exist in life, those that you have no control over such as deaths, job loss, health problems, etc. and those that you may have been instrumental in creating, such as relationship failures, job demotions, foreclosure on your home, etc. When lows happen, you will experience a dip in your path of life. This is a painful time for you, and it requires a great deal of inner strength, and at times help from others, to lift yourself out of these dips. Learning from these lows and introducing new disciplines, attitudes and goals, will be discussed in future steps, which will assist you in pulling yourself out of these dips.

4. **STOP POINTS.** Having the courage and strength to stop the downward trend is necessary to avoid hitting bottom, or better said, avoid a crash and burn scenario. You now need to stabilize yourself, find a balance to your situation and regain a clear vision of where you want to be. Once armed with a clear vision you can again focus on your goals and discipline yourself to stay on track. More discussion will be given to disciplines and attitudes that will be tools to assist in raising you from these dips in life.

5. **CRASH AND BURN.** This happens when you allow a downward trend to continue beyond the stopping point. If a low (dip) gets out of hand, it can produce so much damage in your life that your ability to recover is severely impaired. We will cover the crash and burn scenario in depth later in this step.

Well, there you have it—the five elements to a full cycle in the path of life. We will refer to these elements throughout the book and our workbook. Now that you have been exposed to them, you can think about where you are in relationship to your present cycle. Once you determine this, you can perhaps bring about some needed changes in your attitude, how you react to things, or even how you think. You may be noticing a subtle difference in your thinking already.

Let me share with you a period of time in my life when I experienced both highs and lows (dips), with an end result that made a huge impact on my life. It was an experience that reinforced to me the importance of positive thinking and perseverance even when the odds are stacked against you. This is to help prepare you both for an exercise later in this step, but more importantly, to help you in acknowledging and addressing your path of life's highs and lows (dips).

Dennis' Story

I remember the time in my life when I had achieved my goal of becoming a store manager for a regional grocery chain in Buffalo, New York. My next goal was to become a grocery buyer as outlined in my first ten-year plan (which we will discuss writing ten year plans in Step 3). Every 6 months I knocked on the door of the head buyer for procurement, for this regional grocery chain, to remind him of my interest in becoming a buyer. At this point in time, I was at a plateau as a store manager, trying to move up and over to my next high point. It just wasn't happening for me at this particular time with this company.

So I decided to fly to Phoenix in an attempt to secure a position with another firm that would allow me to attain my goal. However, one of life's lows struck me before I could even get on the plane. I ruptured a disc in my lower spine and was flat on my back for the next twelve weeks. I could barely move and had to sleep on the living room floor. I remember staring at the dots on the stucco ceiling, wondering and worrying about where I was headed. It was definitely at a low point in my path of life.

Then one day as I was laying on the floor, I received a phone call from the personnel department of my company asking if I would be interested in interviewing for a grocery buyer's position that had just become available. My 18 months of persistent door-knocking had finally paid off! The focus I had placed on my desired goal was making my dream come true. There was one significant problem. With my ruptured disc problem, I could not get up and walk to the front door—much less walk into a job interview.

Supported by my wife Patricia, we resolved not to let this opportunity slip through our hands. We set up a time and date for the job interview. When the day arrived, I took my pain medication and Patricia hooked up four electrical wires from a Transcutaneous Electrical Nerve Stimulator unit that the Physical Therapist lent me for my lower back. I felt like a mutant from outer space, but at least the electrical current that ran through the wires killed the pain. After putting on a business suit, I literally crawled out the front door to the van. Then I laid down in the back part of the van while my wife drove me to the interview. By the time we arrived at corporate headquarters, the pain medication had kicked in. I turned the electrical current up to high and went into the interview.

One week later, I was offered the grocery buyer position. We were ecstatic! Now we could dismiss all our thoughts of moving to Phoenix and I could continue moving up the corporate career ladder with a good company. I looked forward to achieving new highs on my path of life, after coming off a substantial low point.

The essence of this story is, there are *dips* in life that are completely unavoidable. I characterize dips as both psychological and tangible. The psychological aspect of dips has to do with changing mindsets and beliefs, effecting how you are feeling emotionally. A tangible dip is the result of an unfortunate incident. What's important is how you react to these dips. For instance, there are still times when I'm on a decline, but rather than overreact, I pause and reflect on the situation. The key is not to get depressed nor take any action that will compound the difficulty of your situation.

In fact, when you are experiencing a low point, it's probably best to avoid any significant decisions. Rather, readjust your thinking to be clear and focused, regaining perspective of a positive state of mind. Then you can analyze your situation to determine steps needed to advance to your next high point.

As Richard Carlson points out in his book, *"You Can Be Happy No Matter What,"* "with an understanding of moods, we can learn to be appreciative of our 'highs' and graceful in our 'lows.' This contrasts sharply with what most of us do in a low mood—where we try to 'think,' 'figure,' or force our way out of it. But you can't force your way out of a low mood any more than you can force yourself to have a good time doing something you don't like. The more force (or thought) you put into it, the lower you sink." This principle applies to solving problems as well.

When you have a clear vision of where you are headed, you will instinctively know what is required of you to reach the next level and you will discipline yourself to do so. Every time you hit a new high point, you will know that getting there was due to the fact that you had a clear focus of where you were going, and the disciplines that allowed you to take the necessary steps to get there.

There are risks involved in upward mobility. These risks include an increase in your personal complacency that can distract your attention away from your "focus and disciplines". The key, as you are moving up, is not to forget this. As much as you may be feeling good about your success in your life at any given moment, this situation can change abruptly if you allow yourself to be distracted.

Discipline must not be confused with obedience. It is not something you are told you must do. It is something you know you must practice. It is, in fact, the stones which pave the way to excellence.
~ Arthur Mitchell, Famous Ballet Director & Choreographer

Maximum Return

Everyone should strive for the ability to achieve highs. The key to these up and down swings in your life's cycles is your staying power at the top of the upswings. How long can you keep and maintain the balance to stay on top? At times you may feel like an aerialist or acrobat balancing the tightrope in a circus performance, but the longer you can maintain your balance and stay on top, the more benefits you will receive. Ralph Waldo Emerson said it this way, *"Our greatest glory is not in never failing, but in rising up every time we fail."*

If you can stay focused on your next set of goals and avoid life's distractions, you will yield maximum return, disproportionately more than time spent in lows.

Crash and Burn

If you have ever flown an airplane, you know how important it is to keep a steady hand on the controls and your eye on the horizon. During take-off, you gather up speed, pull back on the throttle and soar into the sky. Sometimes you encounter turbulence and the plane wobbles around a bit, or you hit an air pocket and lose altitude. It's a lot like the dips you experience in life. Your challenge is not to let the dips get out of hand. In other words, avoid the crash and burn scenario at all costs.

Learn to regulate the amount of dips you have in your life. You may not have a control tower out there guiding you at all times, so you will need to foresee when the dips are coming as often as you can. For example, you are traveling at an altitude of 10,000 feet and you want to get to a higher altitude—say, 30,000 feet. In order to get to an altitude of 30,000 feet or higher, you will need to master how. When you reach a certain level you might need to reduce your speed to the next level without hitting any bumps, or dips.

Many times in life, it is advantageous to slow down your pace— otherwise you will end up in the crash and burn mode. Before you get to that point, it may be required that you stop and re-focus to halt the downward trend. This is when you need to recapture a clear vision of what you are trying to accomplish and what your definition of success is. It will take a fair amount of work and discipline on your part to get back up there and onto the next new high.

Everyone Makes Mistakes—Some More Serious Than Others

A good example of a crash and burn victim is O.J. Simpson. At one time, he was the perfect role model and a lot of people looked up to him. He was the first choice in the 1969 NFL draft and he spent eleven successful years in the NFL. Without doubt he was one of the most popular players in the history of football; he was an actor, sportscaster and the spokesman for Hertz.

I lived in Buffalo, New York during O.J.'s glory years and watched many of his great games. I enjoyed his peak years along with thousands of other Buffalo fans. O.J. had a path in life that went straight up to what many aspire to and classify as sheer success. Unfortunately, he took a dive so extreme that he will most likely never recover from his crash and burn experience. Excerpted from Biography.com *"O.J. Simpson had a successful college football career at USC, winning the Heisman Trophy, Simpson went on to star in the NFL as a running back. He left football in 1979 to pursue what would become a relatively successful acting and commentating career. However, Simpson is now best remembered for his arrest and trial in the 1994 murder of his former wife, Nicole Brown Simpson, and her friend, Ron Goldman, of which he was found not guilty. He is currently in prison for kidnapping and armed robbery convictions that he received in 2008".*

A lack of clear goals or poorly chosen goals, along with inadequate focus and a shortage of discipline, is often times the reason why people get into crash and burn situations. Their ability to stop dips is limited by their unclear focus and their inability to develop self-control and clear thinking.

Another reason could be a fear of success. Fear of success is highly prevalent in the United States. According to an article in *Fortune* magazine, "The dread of doing well in life is rooted deep in the unconscious. Nobody deliberately sets out to wreck his or her own career. And people are so adept at rationalizing their own mistakes, or misinterpreting those of others, that fear of success can be hard to distinguish from . . . incompetence, arrogance, inattention, burnout, or any of the 101 other gremlins that can send a career into a tailspin. . . .' People who have an unconscious fear of success won't set ambitious goals for themselves, so they achieve far less than they're capable of,' says James O'Connell, a psychologist at the outplacement firm Drake Beam Morin. 'And this is the tragedy of it, because ultimately it stops people from getting what they really want or even from asking for help'."

Some people never set goals. They seem to go through life blindfolded, letting others make decisions for them so they never have to take responsibility for their actions. This is reflected in the Nathaniel Brandon book *"The Art of Living Consciously,"* where he states the following: "Living consciously is a state of being mentally active rather than passive. It is the ability to look at the world with fresh eyes. It is intelligence taking joy in its own function. Living consciously is seeking to be aware of everything that bears on our interests, actions, values, purposes, and goals. It is the willingness to confront facts, pleasant or unpleasant. It is the desire to discover our mistakes and correct them. . . ."

There are many possible paths in life that one might journey on. It is our goal to help you chart your path of life. This will lead into observations and implications which will assist you in making changes in your behavior to aid you in achieving success.

TAKEAWAYS: Your Path of Life

- When you understand the five elements of the cycles of life (your highs, lows, plateaus, stopping points and crash & burn scenario), you can create your own personal path of life.

- Once you identify your path of life, you can create a clearer vision of where you have been.

- You will recognize a pattern of behavior that creates your highs and lows, which will allow you to make the necessary changes in your behavior going forward.

- Reaching new highs and staying on top for as long as possible will provide you with the maximum return.

- To avoid crash and burn situations, it is imperative that you take the controls and STOP the downward spiral.

Ambition is the path to success, persistence is the vehicle that you arrive in.
~ Bill Bradley, Former U.S. Senator

Exercise #2A: Your Path of Life

Objective:
- To capture your highs and lows on a life cycle chart to reflect on your life's patterns and identify repeated problems to avoid and/or highs to strive for.

Steps:
- Determine the time period you want to capture on your life cycle chart. The time period will defer for everyone. It is suggested that you use the period of time with the most changes, both negative and positive, to capture your potential learnings. If you have a minimum of ten years or more, that would be recommended to get the full benefit of this exercise. Use additional charts for longer periods of time.

- Identify the high and low points based on your events in your life and determine where they fall on the chart.

- Place a dot on the chart for each high and low period, along with any plateaus.

- Cite any stop points or crash and burns, if they apply to you.

- Once the chart is plotted, then connect your dots to see your path of life. Refer to the chart for example purposes only.

ACHIEVING SUCCESS

EXAMPLE: Your Path of Life: Identify your HIGHS and LOWS in Your Life Cycle

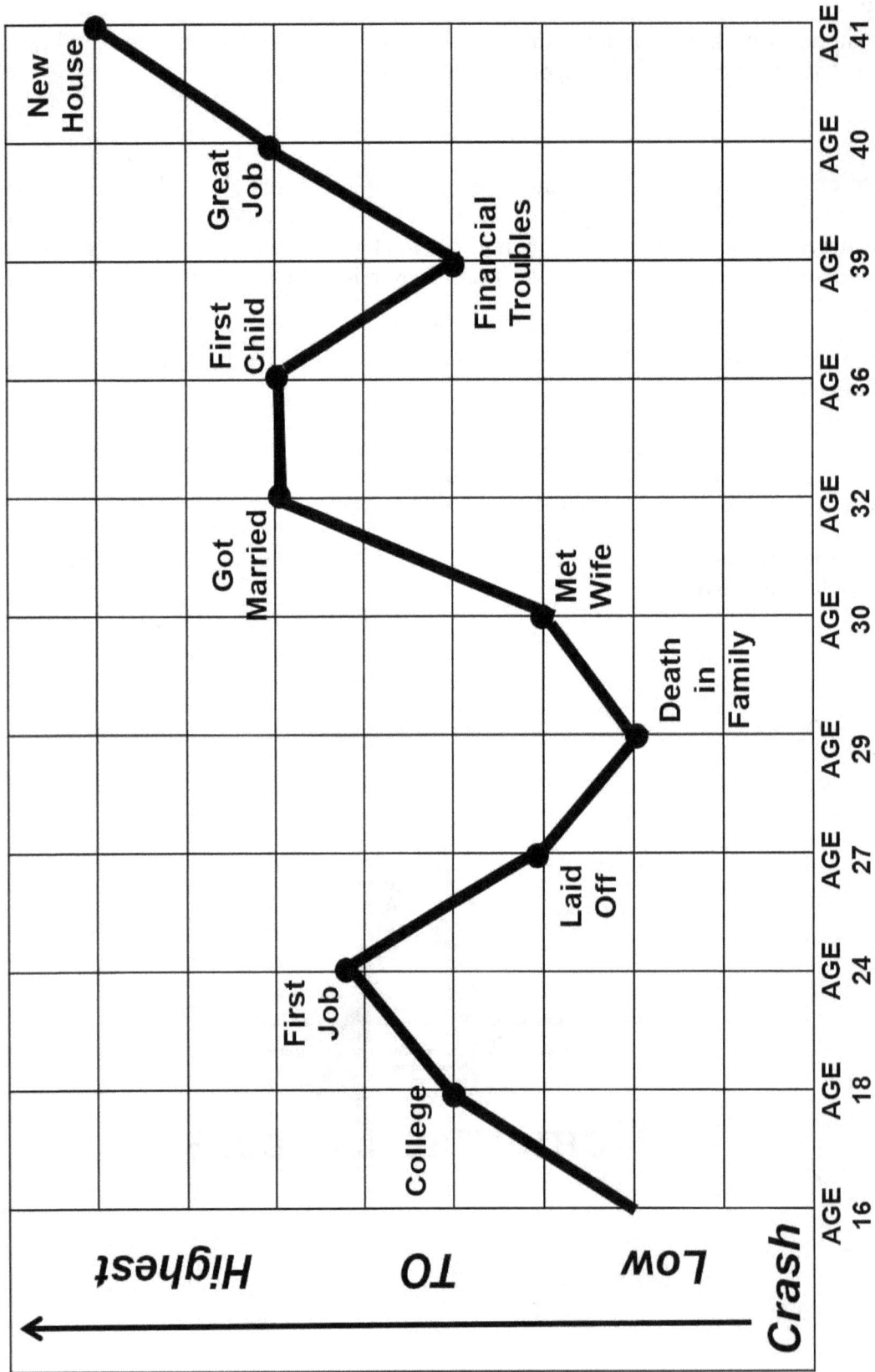

Highest — TO — Low

Crash

| AGE 16 | AGE 18 | AGE 24 | AGE 27 | AGE 29 | AGE 30 | AGE 32 | AGE 36 | AGE 39 | AGE 40 | AGE 41 |

College — First Job — Laid Off — Death in Family — Met Wife — Got Married — First Child — Financial Troubles — Great Job — New House

Your Path of Life: Identify your **HIGHS and LOWS** in Your Life Cycle

Highest

TO

Low

Crash

AGE ___
AGE ___
AGE ___
AGE ___
AGE ___
AGE ___
AGE ___
AGE ___
AGE ___
AGE ___
AGE ___

Your Path of Life: Identify your HIGHS and LOWS in Your Life Cycle

Highest — TO — Low — Crash

AGE AGE AGE AGE AGE AGE AGE AGE AGE AGE AGE

Your Path of Life: Identify your HIGHS and LOWS in Your Life Cycle

Highest

TO

Low

Crash

AGE ___ AGE ___ AGE ___ AGE ___ AGE ___ AGE ___ AGE ___ AGE ___ AGE ___ AGE ___ AGE ___ AGE ___

TESTIMONIAL

Cecilia Bracamontes Ley,

Director of Human Resources, Casa Ley

We worked with Dennis Sobotka and his Life and Career Success Seminar for about 4 years, always with great results. These workshops really helped our people to develop their team and individual skills, by building their own Ten Years Life & Career Plans using new tools and methods learned during the seminars.

Our people started to use these new tools in their jobs with great results. We received a lot of feedback from the people who took the Seminar with Dennis, in which they told us that the new knowledge acquired help them on their jobs, but also on their personal life. And we believe that when an employee improves their personal and family life that have a positive impact on their job tasks.

Casa Ley is very thankful to Dennis for his commitment with our cause, professionalism and for giving our people a wider horizon, sharing new tools to improve their way of thinking.

Once you've completed the chart, the next step is to document any observations that you see in your path of life. Also, write down any consequences of actions that might surface from your observations.

The purpose of these observations is to recognize a pattern of repetition, as many people repeat the same type of negative behavior in their lives. The same can also be said about successful people of repeating the positive behavior that leads to their reaching new highs. By making these observations it generates an understanding of your life pattern and identifies behavioral changes needed.

Questions to explore include, what did you learn about yourself? What periods in your life reflect highs, and what may be the common factors that can be repeated? Are there positive patterns, such as preparedness for work or school, positive work environment, exercising leadership qualities, profitable investments, good financial decisions, commitment to relationships, etc.?

Are you repeating a pattern of behavior that has a negative influence in your life? Examples of negative behaviors can be drinking too much, use of drugs, gambling, lateness at work, overspending, being unfaithful, etc.

This honest reflection of reality in a person's life is rare for most individuals. This type of exercise is intended to facilitate personal insight and changed behavior where needed.

When you lose something in your life, stop thinking it's a loss for you...
it is a gift you have been given so you can get on the right path
to where you are meant to go, not to where you think you should have gone.
~ Suze Orman, Author, Speaker

Exercise #2B: Life's Observations and Corrective Actions

Objective:

- To capture your observations from your path of life and identify actions required to direct your path to meet your goals.

Steps:

- What do you observe happening during your highs/upswings and your lows/dips?

- What happens while you are at a plateau?

- Were you able to impose the stop points?

- Hopefully you have not experienced "crash and burn," but if you have, what did you observe or learn from it?

- What are the consequences of what you observed? What did you learn about yourself? Are there positive patterns? Are you repeating a pattern of behavior that is a negative influence in your life?

- After each observation define corrective action steps that should be taken.

Example: Life Observations & Corrective Actions

List OBSERVATIONS (What do you see?)	List ACTIONS (What corrective action should you take?)
Reoccurring back problems, poor health	Daily exercises and stretches to prevent
Loss of money due to risk taking in market	Invest only in conservative long term funds
Deaths among family members/friends	Spend more time with aging family & friends
Family growing – expenses increasing	Budget needs for growing expenses
Cars keep breaking down	Trade in cars every 5 years to be proactive
Repetitive cycle of alcoholic drinking	Need outside help to overcome addiction
Repetitive cycle of drug use, arrested & jail	Need outside help to overcome addiction
Divorced three times, I'm the problem	I need to change my attitude & behavior
Several job promotions, focus & disciplined	Repeat and maintain
Won significant games, used visualization	Continue and expand using visualization

Life Observations & Corrective Actions

List OBSERVATIONS (What do you see?)	List ACTIONS (What corrective action should you take?)

TESTIMONIAL

Elizabeth Porterfield, MS, MS.Ed., LMHC
New York State Certified School Counselor

"Having collaborated with Dennis Sobotka for over a decade, I am thrilled that he is sharing his incredible knowledge. Working in a large urban school district and serving students with diverse language proficiencies, cultures, and experiences, I have witnessed how Mr. Sobotka's program, "Achieving Life and Career Success" has encouraged adolescent students identify priorities, challenges, and dreams.

This highly organized system has resulted in clearly defined future plans, strong self-confidence, and healthy relationships with self and others. Whether 15 years old or 50, anyone and everyone's life can be improved and enriched by incorporating Dennis' methods for setting direction, accepting personal responsibility, and spending time with intention.

If you're looking for a structure and techniques designed to support the creation of meaning and happiness, Dennis Sobotka's approach is for you."

SWOT

SWOT stands for our personal **S**trengths, **W**eaknesses, **O**pportunities, and **T**hreats. You now need to review your path of life's highs and lows, recognizing that in most cases, but not always, your highs reflect your strengths and your lows are related to one or more of your weaknesses. Your strengths and weaknesses are considered internal measures while the opportunities and threats are external factors. You need to acknowledge and leverage your strengths when future opportunities come along, especially those requiring personal commitment or measurable results. You need to acknowledge and correct our weaknesses so you avoid future threats, such as being passed over for a promotion or getting fired from a job, not meeting your project deadline, being unreliable for those you care about, getting a divorce, etc. Working from your path of life observations and corrective actions, start to identify all of your strengths. Then repeat this for your weaknesses. Once those are complete, define what might be future opportunities and threats based on these strengths and weaknesses.

TAKEAWAYS: Your SWOT

- Documenting your strengths encourages you to leverage your opportunities

- Be honest with yourself when recording your weaknesses to avoid future threats in life.

- By defining your SWOT, you can balance your life with more emphasis on your strengths and opportunities and reduce time and energy on your weaknesses and threats.

My attitude is that if you push me towards something that you think is a weakness,
then I will turn that perceived weakness into a strength.
~ Michael Jordan, Former Basketball Player & Businessman

Exercise #2C: Your SWOT

Objective:
- To leverage your strengths and seize your opportunities while improving on weaknesses and protecting against your threats.

Steps:
- Write your internal strengths.

- Write your external opportunities that reflect your internal strengths.

- Write your internal weaknesses.

- Write your external threats that could or have developed due to your weaknesses.

Build your weaknesses until they become your strengths
~ Knute Rockne, Coach, Author, Football Player

Example: YOUR Personal SWOT

STRENGTHS: (Internal)

1. Good communicator
2. Problem solving
3. Positive & pleasant personality
4. Creative
5. Well organized

WEAKNESSES: (Internal)

6. Loss of money due to risk taking in market
7. Divorced three times, I'm the problem
8. Poor communication & relationships
9. Reoccurring back problems, poor health
10. Repetitive cycle of alcoholic drinking

OPPORTUNITIES: (External)

1. Leadership positions in career
2. Help others in the family and in career
3. Finding wonderful spouse & friends
4. Add innovation into every situation
5. Able to handle multiple tasks, job advancement

THREATS: (External)

6. In debt & could go bankrupt
7. End up alone & lonely in life
8. Divorce & decreased income
9. Losing mobility, loss of job & income
10. Loss of job & income, poor health & death

YOUR Personal SWOT

OPPORTUNITIES: (External)

1.
2.
3.
4.
5.

THREATS: (External)

6.
7.
8.
9.
10.

STRENGTHS: (Internal)

1.
2.
3.
4.
5.

WEAKNESSES: (Internal)

6.
7.
8.
9.
10.

STEP 3

Your Ten Year Goals
"Where are You Going?"

SEVEN STEPS (7)

Odyssey of
Learning

Cloud of
Unknowing

Creative
Visualization

Attitudes
Disciplines

**Step 3: YOUR
TEN YEAR GOALS**

Your Path
of Life

Define
Success

People with goals succeed because they know where they're going.
~ Earl Nightingale, Radio Personality, Speaker & Author

You have completed your work in defining "Where Have You Been?" and identified your personal SWOT. With this base of learning, you can move forward to discuss "Where Are You Going?" Below is an outline of what is covered in Step 3 of the 7 Step Process:

The Hierarchy of this 7 Step Process: The hierarchy used in this process starts and ends with your definition of success completed in Step 1. Step 3 introduces long term goals which you will establish into a ten year plan. These ten year goals will be broken down into short term goals to make them manageable and measureable. As you proceed on your path to success, you will strive for individual milestones, which will vary from person to person. These milestones should represent completion of significant phases in your individual ten year plan. You will know your journey is complete upon reaching your definition of success.

1. **Ten Year Goals**: As the title infers, you will be setting goals, both short-term and long-term goals. The long-term goals (ten year goals) will be discussed first, which may seem unusual, however explanation is provided in understanding that long range forecasting is encouraged before developing your short-term measurable goals. Examples of ten year planning are shared, and specifically, career planning is highlighted. There will be exercises presented for defining both personal and career ten year goal setting.

2. **Career Ladder**: Defining a Career Ladder is discussed at length as an example of goal setting and encouragement for career growth. This is just one of many areas of individual planning but a specific need that is shared by most readers.

3. **Short-term goals** (one year goal setting) are introduced after establishing ten year goals and an exercise is presented to assist you in developing these goals. Your short-term goals need to be measurable and designed to reach your long-term ten year goals, therefore are developed after your long range forecasting.

4. **Priority Planning** on a daily, weekly, monthly basis is an ongoing action step to fulfilling your one year goals. These priorities are discussed and a worksheet provided to help you establish new priorities.

5. **Mission Statement**: The last component of Step 3 is developing your own personal mission statement. Your mission statement should be a reflection of your life's purpose and motivate you towards your long term goals.

Many components are included in Step 3, all with the same objective, to help define "Where are You Going?" These components should result in a successful life plan.

Setting Goals

"Goooal!" Soccer fans will recognize the famous cheer of the U.S. Women's National Soccer Team when they defeated Japan 5-2 to become the 2015 FIFA Women's World Cup Champions. What an accomplishment! Just as the Women's Soccer Team accomplished the goal of winning the World Cup, everyone should look upon reaching goals as a significant part of their path to success. Most of us live each day by giving ourselves small tasks to complete. Perhaps you keep a "to do" list at your desk or pasted on the refrigerator door. You probably check off the items on this list as you complete them.

Your "to do" list is precise. It tells you that you need to finish a report, make phone calls to certain people, write your business report, pick up the dry cleaning on your way home from the office, etc.

Goals, too, must be precise. When asked what their goals are, some people who attend our success seminars say things like: "I want to make more money," "I'd like to have more control over my business," "My goal is to get more notoriety in my field." Trying to achieve "more" in this sense can be very difficult. It's too vague. You will stand a better chance at reaching your goals if they are clear and precise. Most often the initial goals you dream about are long term goals that require completion of short term goals first, before attaining the ultimate dream. For example, wanting more money may require changing careers, investments, attending workshops, further education, etc., which happens over time.

Specific goals with measurable results are needed to motivate action. Financial planners understand this philosophy which is why they are always talking with their clients about setting financial goals—short-term, mid-term, and longer-term goals. They ask their clients to get really specific about their financial goals. A short-term goal may be to maintain an emergency cash reserve that equals three months' income. A mid-term goal might be to put $60,000 away for a child's education. A long-term goal would likely be to manage financially on interest generated from investments throughout retirement. Setting financial goals is all about taking control of one's financial future one step at a time.

If you are interested in taking control of your life, then setting goals for all aspects of your life is important. Goals are the day-to-day blueprint of your path of life and they help to bring order to your behavior. As you get in the habit of setting goals and reaching them, you will begin naturally to set goals that are more demanding. Before you realize it, you will be reaching goals that are on course for your path to success. Setting goals should be a significant part of your life's plan to success.

The first step towards getting somewhere is to decide that you are not going to stay where you are
~John Pierpont (JP) Morgan, American Financial Banker

Setting Ten-Year Goals First

If you are like most of us, you think in terms of setting goals that are attainable within a short period of time. However there is something more effective about establishing big, long-term goals. Many people plan their lives without consciously doing so, for example, individuals often decide how long they will be engaged before getting married, while also preplanning at what age they may want to start their families. Or for others, they think about where they want to live and how soon they will be able to afford buying a home. Long term planning should be a conscious commitment with complete written detail.

You can apply this simple principle of establishing time frames when setting both career and personal goals. One tends to think in terms of three months to three years at most however you should establish significant ten-year goals. There are many benefits to thinking in ten-year increments. First of all, ten years is a relatively long time and you can accomplish many things during this period of time.

Also, there is no immediate pressure to accomplish everything at once when you set long-term goals. You don't want to get overwhelmed, instead you want to believe it's achievable. If you place your goals too close to the present, chances are you may begin to feel anxious and uncertain about reaching them. You have to give yourself the time to create the steps you need to realize your goals.

We have encouraged you to think big and define your success based on your dreams. You will need big goals to reach your success, however, to reach these big goals, you need to start with short-term goals. We encourage using these short term measurable goals that will build towards achieving your 10 year goals. Take one step at a time so that you recognize your accomplishments which encourages you to continue to strive for longer termed goals. Therefore, establish the long term goals and then work towards them with short term, measurable goals.

The following example highlights this process using this methodology of short-term measureable goals. Let's say you have a fear of heights but you have a goal to go skydiving with your spouse. How would you approach preparing yourself for this event with short-term measurable goals? Start with accomplishing a task that requires climbing a ladder in a familiar place, which will be your first measurable result. Using visualization to prepare yourself emotionally for climbing the ladder is recommended. Visualization will be discussed in depth in step 5. Once that feat is accomplished, you then move on to climbing to the top of a building, looking over the city. Each step brings you to a higher point of accomplishment, with the end result of overcoming the fear of heights. Now you decide you are ready to skydive. You have to become acquainted with the equipment, exit procedure, canopy steering, landings, etc. Building on this step by step and preparing for this activity, you can be successful using short-term, measurable goals. We encourage you to celebrate each accomplishment along the way. Although it may seem small, it is each small accomplishment that will get you to your larger goals therefore providing yourself positive reinforcement is important.

Your plan for the future must be definable and measurable. Sometimes it is simply a matter of the amount of time you give yourself to realize your objectives. For example, when you graduate from high school at the age of eighteen, it is probably not realistic to think that in ten years you could become president of the United States. Given everything that you would need to accomplish, it is just not practical, but it would be feasible to put together two ten-year plans to strive for this notable goal. You would start with the first ten-year plan to achieve the goal of possibly becoming mayor of a small city. To achieve this first ten-year goal using the methodology of measurable short-term goals, you might lay out one-year plans as follows:

FIRST TEN-YEAR PLAN

YEAR	ACTIVITY
1st and 2nd years	Attend college, participate in student council.
3rd and 4th years	Attend college, work part-time in local government and on local campaigns.
5th and 6th years	Get a job in politics and learn the realities of how government works.
7th year	Run for local government position and win.
8th year	Remain in office and make a significant contribution to the community.
9th year	Run for mayor of the city and win.
10th year	Remain in office and improve the quality of life in your community.

With the achievement of your first ten-year plan under your belt, you would lay out your second ten-year plan with the same approach. This ten-year plan might resemble the following:

SECOND TEN-YEAR PLAN

YEAR	ACTIVITY
1st year	Run for state legislator and win.
2nd year	Continue in office and pass a few major bills.
3rd year	Run for state senator and win.
4th year	Continue in office and pass a few major bills.
5th year	Run for governor of your state and win.
6th and 7th years	As governor, put your state on the map in a big way.
8th and 9th years	As governor, build a national platform to run for president of the U.S.,
10th year	Run for U.S. president and win.

Believe it or not, former President Clinton followed a similar route to the two ten year plans just listed. It has been written that as a young man in Arkansas, Bill Clinton dreamed about (visualized) being a president much like John F. Kennedy, who happened to be his role model. Clinton went through a number of government positions, became governor of the state of Arkansas, and then went on to become one of the youngest presidents of our nation. Granted, it's an exceedingly simplified version of the path Clinton took, but the point is well made, measurable short-term goals.

This example relates to one area in Clinton's life, his political aspirations. However ten year plans should be broader in scope to capture more components in your life that will run parallel with other goals. For instance, your family life will be shaped within a ten year plan and goals to maintain or increase family size is admirable. Many people today consider health issues to be crucial in their planning for longevity and healthy living. Career goals, travel desires, and living residences are all goals that would run parallel to each other, different issues but during the same time frame.

Ten-year plans give you time to fill in huge voids of knowledge, experience, and maturity to accomplish many seemingly impossible goals. People usually think ten years is too long a time to plan for. After all, many things can change as time goes on—and that's true. Equally true, however, is that with no ten-year plan time marches on, and the opportunity to identify and gain the knowledge and skills you need to reach your goals is often missed. With a plan, even if you are able to accomplish 30, 50 or 80 percent of your plan, you are that much farther ahead.

My intent here is to have you recognize that a ten year plan should be all encompassing and a program that generates a balanced life. This leads into our next section and exercise, developing a well-balanced ten year plan.

Developing a Ten Year Plan

Do you have a ten year plan for achieving your goals? When you put down a clear vision of what you want to accomplish in your life, you are better equipped to take advantage of opportunities when they arise. This is true on both an individual and on a family level.

When I was young, I didn't understand the power of setting big aggressive goals. Eventually though, I understood that when you set goals, your subconscious mind helps to make them happen. This is true even on a daily basis; each little action that you take or small decision you make brings you closer to your goals. And if you write them down in detail, they indeed occur more precisely and clearly.

When considering a ten year plan, it is helpful to take time for quiet reflection. While reflecting on your future, practice visualizing in your mind what would bring you success in ten years. Step 1 has already prepared you for this next exercise by defining your definition of success. Review your definition of success and transfer the individual subject goals into a ten year plan. You need to determine where you should be in ten years in relationship to your ultimate dream of success. Remember that identifying measurable goals over a ten year period will position you for success.

Try sharing your goals with others. This can be especially helpful if you are a procrastinator. I can't tell you how many times in my life I have done something simply because I told someone I was going to do it. There are a couple of things that work psychologically when you do this. First of all, you feel embarrassed when the person you confided in confronts you with the question, "Well, did you do that thing you told me you were going to do?" and you haven't even put much thought into it. And secondly, verbalizing your goal to another person imprints it in your subconscious mind.

Now let's begin creating your ten year plan in Exercise 3A. In this exercise you will address all aspects of your life, including your career. Take into consideration that the second exercise, 3B is dedicated to just your career planning in much more detail. In Exercise 3A, you will notice there are two worksheets, one which captures the "core" ten year plan and the second which offers a more "expanded" ten year plan. Using both will help you achieve your success in life.

TAKEAWAYS: Ten and One Year Goals

- You need a clear idea of where you want to be in your life ten years from now. Record your ten-year goals and visualize them in your mind. Focus on attaining these goals.

- Ten years gives you time to fill in significant voids of knowledge, experience, and maturity to accomplish seemingly impossible goals.

- Achieving long-term success is the result of setting short-term goals and reaching them, therefore, it is important to set one-year goals. They are the steps you take to finally obtain that pot of gold at the end of your rainbow, your ten year goals.

You must have long term goals to keep you from being frustrated by short term failures.
~ Charles C. Noble, Nobel-Prize-Winning Irish Playwright

Exercise #3A: Your Ten Year "Life" Goal Setting

Objective:

- Document your ten year goals to achieve your dreams of success.

Steps:

- Begin your planning with the "core" example worksheet. Start by identifying what subjects are important to you in your life and then list them in the left hand column titled "subject".

- For each subject listed, identify the goal, why it is important, how you will complete it and when (time frame) will it be done.

- This provides you with a well charted game plan for your next ten years. Some people may decide to stop here and work from this basic plan.

- However, now that you have a foundation for your ten year plan, we urge you to continue your planning by using the more "expanded" example that will lead you through yearly actions that will reach your goals.

- Before filling in the columns, you need to complete the headers at the top, which are the years broken down over a ten year period and your corresponding age to each year.

- Once that is done, you now will refer to your core plan and take the first subject you listed and place it in the left column. Then go to the last column, ten year, and fill in what the ten year goal is for that particular subject. Repeat this for all other subjects you have listed.

- Now you are going to work backwards to complete each year, one through nine, with actions required that will move you closer to your ten year goal. Remember to use measurable short-term goals each year.

- When completed, reflect on what you have listed and make any adjustments that will secure reaching your ten year goals.

CORE Example

YOUR TEN YEAR GOALS
Ages: 18-27   Years: 2015 - 2024

SUBJECT	GOALS	WHY	HOW	WHEN (Timeframe)
Education / Personal Development	Graduate college with MBA	Land a high paying professional job.	Study hard to get 3.5 GPA.	Complete first 4 yrs with BA.
Career	Career in business	Desire to work financial services.	Internships with financial institutions during college. Network with business organizations and people.	Upon graduation.
Relationship	Marry before I turn 30.	Desire an everlasting love & have a family.	Spend time & learn all about him/her; know he/she loves me for who I am.	After college & when in love.
Family	Plan for children	Important to have them always in my life.	Ongoing contact and quality time while visiting.	Visit at least monthly.
Location	Buy duplex in LA	Want to live in LA for weather and jobs.	Secure a good paying job to afford LA expenses. Degree with assure this.	Upon graduation
Mentors Role Models	Business & spiritual mentors & role models	For faster progress in career & spirituality.	Seek out & ask exceptional people for their mentorship. Research role models	Each year of the ten year plan.
Financial	Save for duplex	Income & equity for future expenditures.	Develop a monthly savings program & stick to it.	Buy duplex by year ten.
Vacation	Honeymoon to Hawaii	Always wanted to see Hawaii but never could.	Save $100 each month until I have enough for this trip.	After college loans are paid.

YOUR TEN YEAR GOALS

CORE Worksheet

Years:

Ages:

SUBJECT	GOALS	WHY	HOW	WHEN (Timeframe)

EXPANDED Example — YOUR TEN YEAR GOALS

SUBJECT	1	2	3	4	5	6	7	8	9	10
Year	2015	2016	2017	2018	2019	2020	2021	2022	2023	2024
Age	18	19	20	21	22	23	24	25	26	27
Education / Personal Development	Enroll in college / BS degree	College major in business	College major in business	College major in business Graduate	Graduate BA & start masters program	Masters program MBA	Personal growth	Personal growth	Personal growth	Graduate college with MBA
Career	PT night manager	PT night manager	PT night manager	PT night manager	Financial internship	Financial internship	1st career position	1st career position	1st career position	Career in business
Relationship	Date different people	Date different people	Develop relation-ship	Develop relation-ship	Find right person	Find right person	Talk marriage	Get engaged	Plan wedding	Marry before I turn 30.
Family	Monthly visits	Monthly visits	Monthly visits	Monthly visits	Monthly visits	Monthly visits	Visit 3x year	Visit 3x year	Visit 3x year	Plan for children
Location	Away at College	College dorm	College dorm	College dorm	College dorm	First apartment	Move to LA - rent	Rent in LA	Rent in LA	Buy duplex in LA
Mentors Role Models	College professor	College professor	College professor	College professor	Manager	Manager	Boss	Boss	Spiritual guide	Business & spiritual mentors
Financial	College loan	Buy a car	Pay for car	Pay for college	Pay for college	Buy Furniture	Save for duplex	Save for duplex	Save for duplex	Save for duplex
Vacation	Florida with friends	Camping Fishing	Florida with friends	Camping Fishing	Camping Hiking	Florida & friends	Visit Mexico	Backpack Europe	Backpack Europe	Honeymoon to Hawaii

EXPANDED Worksheet

YOUR TEN YEAR GOALS

SUBJECT	1	2	3	4	5	6	7	8	9	10
Year										
Age										

Ten Year "Career" Ladder Success Planning

Next you will create a second parallel ten year plan dedicated to your career planning. For the majority of employable readers, managing your career is a key component to your ten-year goal planning. With this degree of importance, take additional time to identify what your desirable career ladder is going forward.

When presenting our success seminars, it is our philosophy to encourage you to establish career goals within your existing employer to maximize opportunities within that company or organization. Generally speaking, it is to your advantage, as well as to the employers, to climb the career ladder within your company. Although we encourage growth within your current work environment, we recognize at times individuals will need to change employers to obtain their dreams of success.

I like to relate the following story about how I shared my goals with my wife, Patricia, to illustrate how my first ten-year career plan came about.

Dennis' Ten Year Career Plan

When my wife and I were first married in 1977, we took up cross country skiing. Like many newlyweds, we were young, didn't have a lot of money, and had very little in the way of material things. During one of our skiing excursions we sat down to rest at a picnic table. I began to share with my wife some of my thoughts about our future. In the course of our conversation, I said that although I had just graduated with a degree in marketing and business, it would not mean anything in the "real world." I told her I thought I needed at least three work experiences before I could get to the level I desired.

In my mind, I saw my career path as a three-part journey. First, I wanted to be a retail store manager, then a buyer, and, finally, I envisioned myself as a well-rounded corporate man who would be involved in all aspects of the retail business, a key focal point. I figured it would take me about three years in each position to accomplish what I needed to do. I specifically told my wife that I was going to spend the next ten years of my life attaining these three milestone goals. At the end of this ten-year plan discussion, I told Patricia, I should be a well-rounded corporate person. Then we skied home.

As it happened, I was a store manager for three-and-a-half years, then I was promoted to the buyer's position. After three years as a buyer, I advanced to the position of Grocery Staff Coordinator, a position I held for three-and-a-half years also. In this job, I was responsible for coordinating all procurement and merchandising between ten grocery buyers and fifty-nine stores, which qualified me as a well-rounded business man. With these three positions, I met the big goal I had set ten years earlier. At the end of ten years, I had three different work experiences to my credit, which is exactly what I had set out to do.

Dennis's First 10 Year Plan Example

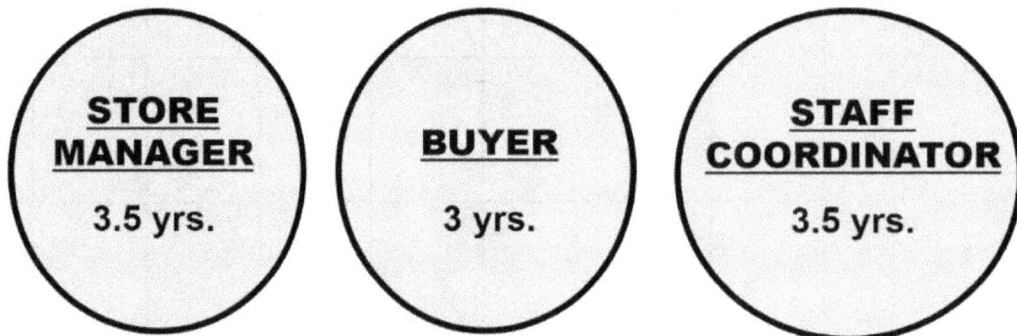

STORE MANAGER	BUYER	STAFF COORDINATOR
3.5 yrs.	3 yrs.	3.5 yrs.

First 10 Year Plan Goals Achieved

At this point, I was offered the position as assistant director of the grocery department at this company. This completed my first ten-year plan and I achieved my objective of becoming a well-rounded business man.

As I look back on that first ten-year plan, which was visualized atop a snow-covered picnic table, I was amazed at what I had accomplished. That is when I understood the power of long-term planning and goal setting. There were many voids of work related expertise that I needed to fill with job experience, and the ten years allowed me to fill them.

> *Determine what specific goal you want to achieve. Then dedicate yourself to its*
> *attainment with unswerving singleness of purpose, the zeal of a crusader.*
> ~ Paul J. Meyer, Motivational Speaker, Author

Let me continue to use my own career example to highlight the importance of career ladder success planning. I worked for a total of 17+ years with the same regional supermarket chain. During those years, I held 5 significant positions that contributed to my overall career success. After my first ten year goals were reached, I developed the next ten year career plan to continue up the ladder becoming the assistant director of the grocery department. I was then promoted to Director of Grocery, overseeing a department with a one billion dollar budget. That milestone of success helped complete my 2nd ten year plan in less time than expected. I did not leave that employer until I felt I had maximized all my opportunities, at which time I left the company to begin my third ten year plan that included a significant career change.

Since each reader will be significantly different due to their age, maturity, and experience, it's hard to give definable direction of your career ladder in this book. However during our success seminars, we are able to give those in attendance personalized feedback and direction. Considering the variables of each reader, let me share the following guidelines and insight when you are designing your personal career ladder.

Guidelines of Career Ladder

In a typical ten year career plan you should strive to achieve 3 significant positions during that time. Now that's not absolute, but it's a strategy that is effective for career development. The purpose of 3 different positions is to broaden your experience to make you more valuable for your future steps in your career path.

You should give yourself 3 years to start and complete each position. Here is an example of how it could play out:

1. The first year is focused on *learning* your new position and gaining respect from your peers and supervisors or bosses.

2. The second year is focused on *mastering* your job responsibilities and delivering value to your company/organization.

3. The third-year is to *expand* the scope of your position, strive to be recognized for your next promotion and train your replacement.

         www.achievingsuccesscenter.com

Each Position: 3 Year Cycles

1st Year
LEARN
My Position

2nd Year
MASTER
My Position

3rd Year
EXPAND
My Position

This process of accomplishment, which may vary in time frame, should be repeated with each new position you acquire within the company. Optimal would be 3 positions within your ten year plan, but again this is not an absolute, rather time frame to work towards.

Potential Career Growth Ladder

3 Year Position
STEP 1
On Ladder

3 Year Position
STEP 2
On Ladder

3 Year Position
STEP 3
On Ladder

⟷

10 YEAR CAREER PLAN

Does this happen to all good employees? No, but it is more likely to happen to the person who has established a ten year success plan and remains committed to working towards those goals. This is a process that will vary from individual to individual, but one thing that is universal, is the need to fill voids of knowledge and experience in order to climb your career ladder of success. When you advance in your career, you may find it necessary to make lateral moves at times. This is not uncommon and often necessary to complete a cycle of experience that is required before you can continue to move up the career ladder. In other words, sometimes you need to concede to lateral moves that don't offer salary increases but offer you the opportunity to fulfill the voids in experience that is needed to qualify you for future vertical positions that will include better pay compensation.

An important variable in your career growth is recognizing your strengths and weaknesses, which we previously discussed your SWOT in Step 2. With confidence, you need to discuss your interest of upward mobility with the human resource department and/or your supervisor. Share with them your desire to learn beyond your specific role and eagerness to attend workshops or educational conferences that will provide for your personal development in related skills and work performance. The sheer fact that you are showing initiative, passion and sincere interest in moving forward are attributes that many employers are looking for in their workforce.

CAREER LADDER

FIRST 10 Year Plan

SECOND 10 Year Plan

THIRD 10 Year Plan

MAJOR Career Goal

Seventh Position

Sixth Position

Fifth Position

Fourth Position

Third Position

Second Position

First Position

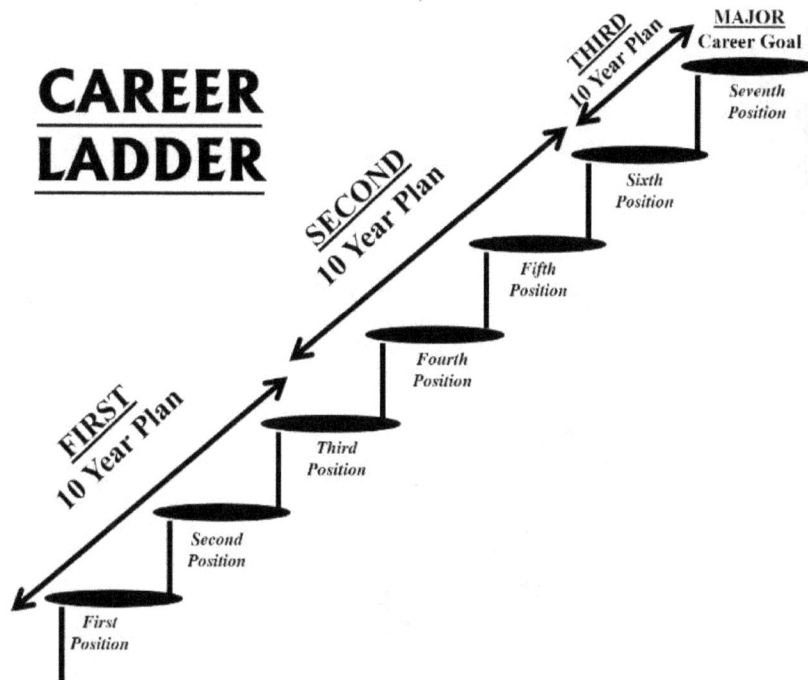

A career ladder will most likely represent more than one ten year plan. Similar to the example of President Clinton's two ten year plans to reach his optimal political aspirations as President, and my two ten year plans to reach the top of my career ladder.

The path to success is to take massive, determined action.
~ Anthony Robbins, Motivational Speaker & Author

Exercise #3B: Your Ten Year "Career" Ladder

Objective:
- Define desired career positions for your career ladder.

Steps:
- Reflect on your company's organizational structure and identify your desired career ladder.
- On each step write the title of your desired position. You may use less or more steps, depending on your goals. You can refer to the example below.
- Once your career ladder is identified, it can be incorporated into your life success plan. The quality time you spend completing your ten year career plan will translate into greater success in your life.

Example:

TEN YEAR
Career Ladder

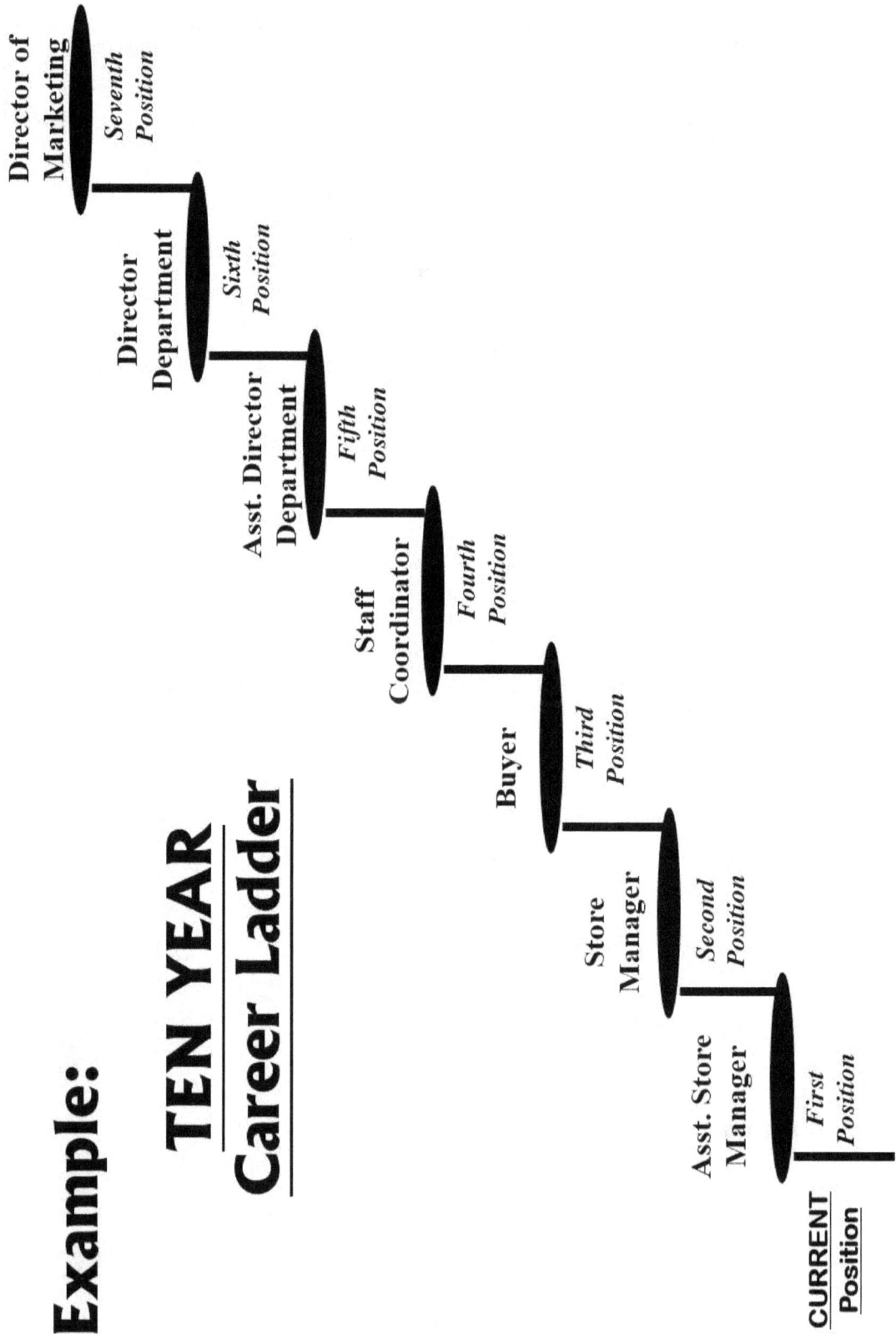

Director of Marketing — *Seventh Position*

Director Department — *Sixth Position*

Asst. Director Department — *Fifth Position*

Staff Coordinator — *Fourth Position*

Buyer — *Third Position*

Store Manager — *Second Position*

Asst. Store Manager — *First Position*

CURRENT Position

TEN YEAR
Career Ladder

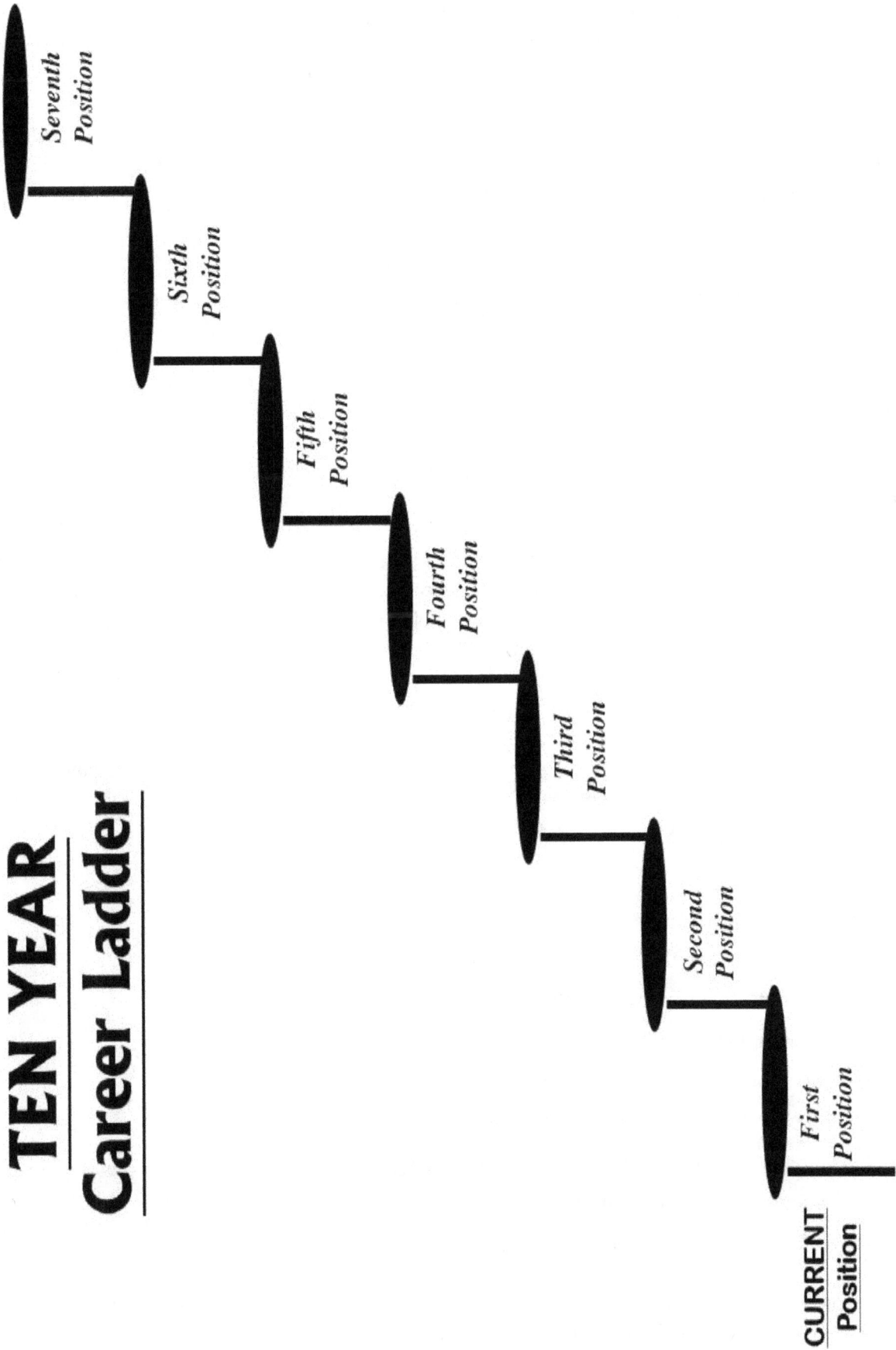

Seventh Position

Sixth Position

Fifth Position

Fourth Position

Third Position

Second Position

First Position

CURRENT Position

Establishing One-Year Goals

As outlined in the first section of this step, one year goals are designed to work towards reaching your ten year goals. Therefore, it makes sense to develop your one year goals after you have established your ten year goals.

No one ever said becoming successful would be easy. Following a process, whether it be at work or in your personal life, will always increase your likelihood to success. Because of the importance of this 7 Step Process, a brief summary of what we have shared up to this point would be helpful.

- Dreaming big was encouraged in establishing long-term goals

- Setting ten year goals will influence your short-term goals

- Reach your long-term goals through achieving your short- term objectives.

It is now time to examine short-term goals. One year goals are very precise with measurable short-term results. These goals need to be very specific to individual tasks to ensure completion. Think smaller tasks within a shorter time frame.

In our seminars, we ask participants to arrange their one-year goals by subject. These subjects may include anything you feel is related to implementing your ten-year plan, such as completing levels of education; obtaining desired job promotion; saving a specific dollar amount; learning a new skill; taking the next step in a relationship; etc.

As you formulate your ten-year plan and outline how you will accomplish your goals, it's important to ask yourself why you are choosing this particular path. Knowing why is important because it is your motivation for implementing the plan. It helps you to stay focused and on track. You will use your one-year goals as stepping stones to complete the ten-year plan.

For example, you have been teaching in the public schools for the past 3 years. You are less excited about teaching and want to reevaluate your career options. In establishing a ten year plan, your dream job would be as a school superintendent of a small school district.

Recognizing that you will need greater leadership skills, administrative experience and other educational credentials, you establish your goals accordingly. What one year career goals would be required to reach your ten year career position as a school superintendent?

Your one year goals could include the following:
- Increase leadership roles

- Continue educational credits in administration

- Attend administrative evening classes

- Chairperson for public school committees

- Involvement in district wide committees

- Attend committees for the national educational organizations

- Participation at conferences and in-services designed for continued educational credits

- Apply for assistant principal positions within 5 years of teaching experience

- Apply for a principal position 3 years after being an assistance principal

These are all one year goals that could be incorporated into your long range plans. A "big dream" for teachers, yet a very realistic goal if developed using the ten year goal setting approach.

Another example, if your goal in ten years is to become a restaurateur and open a four-star restaurant, then using the exercise chart, you might list cooking skills under the **subject category**.

- Under **goal,** you might write down that you would like to learn how to prepare French sauces.
- Next you write down **why** you want to learn this
- Then **how** you will accomplish it.
- **When** you will take the time to do it is important, so write it down as well. Is it a daily, weekly or monthly activity?

Using the French sauce example, you would want to learn how to make this sauce because it would be a requirement in reaching your long-term goal of becoming a restaurateur.

You could take a course in making French sauces at a culinary institute or get a job as a sous-chef under a renowned French chef. As a sous-chef, you would work long hours nearly every day. The culinary class could meet twice a week for twelve weeks, but at the end of either of these activities you will have reached one of your short-term goals.

You may not accomplish all of the one-year goals you set for yourself. Sometimes twelve months just isn't enough time. In today's world, people are constantly looking for instant gratification, a quick fix, or a fast reward for things. They give up if they don't get it fast enough. Giving up is not an option if you want to attain your goals.

No one ever came knocking at my door to hand me the jobs that got me to the finish line in terms of my objectives. To implement my third ten-year plan, I wrote one letter to one person who was the general partner of the company I was looking to work for. In this letter, I told him about my first and second ten-year plans, my areas of expertise and what I had accomplished in these areas. I shared my third ten-year plan that included my participation in his company, along with my expectations and what I thought I could deliver. I knew I wanted a maximum return on my first two ten-year plans. One of my goals was to increase my experience in the manufacturing, distribution and retailing business. Another one of my goals was to travel the world and get paid for doing it. Both goals would be accomplished if offered a job at his company

It wasn't always easy and required long hours and hard work, but I was able to accomplish 100% of my third ten-year plan. I continue to outline yearly goals to accomplish my next ten-year plan.

You too can accomplish your goals. All you need is a clear vision of what you want, a belief in yourself that you can do it, and the self-discipline to work at attaining your short-term goals each year with the measurable results of obtaining your ten-year goals.

The most important thing about goals is having one.
~ Geoffrey F. Abert, Author

TAKEAWAYS: One Year Goals

- Achieving long-term success is the result of setting short-term goals and reaching them, therefore, it is important to set one-year goals. They are the steps you take to finally obtain that pot of gold at the end of your rainbow, your ten year goals.

TESTIMONIAL

***Rosanne G. Inserra, Assistant Superintendent
of Academic Services, Phoenix, Arizona***

"As a Principal and Assistant Superintendent of Academic Services, I see the value of assisting students with a process and graphic organizers to focus their thoughts, reflections and goals. Your well-designed success workbook, "Achieving Life and Career Success," gave those teens an easy structure to follow and continue to use throughout their life.

Many concepts covered in your seminar workshops apply to their future as adults in the workforce. Self-awareness and assurance in their personal lives will be an outcome from this experience. The boys appeared actively involved in each workshop and engaged in the learning activities. Their participation demonstrated the relevance they found in your presentation. To maintain the attention from 24 teenage boys who possess focusing difficulties as well as behavior problems, speaks for itself.

Your personal touch with positive reinforcements and a sense of humor added to the day. Culminating with a certificate added a final touch that documented your sincerity and individualization of this program.

I encourage you to continue with these seminars for children, young teens and adults. You have a great deal of insight and much to offer people who need direction and self-disciplines. Your message is a powerful one."

Exercise #3C: Your One Year Goals

Objective:
- To write your one-year goals.

Steps:
- Using the worksheet provided in this section, write down, in detail, what you want to accomplish for your first year. Address each element on the worksheet. Remember to use specific goals with measurable results.

- Your one-year goals should be established to accomplish your ten-year plan. Continue repeating this process throughout the ten year plan.

One Suggested format:

Subject: List key subjects for this year.

Goals: Next write your goals for each subject.

Why: Write down *why* this goal is important.

How: Then state *how* you will accomplish it.

When: Write down when you will take the time to do it, is it a daily, weekly or monthly activity?

Reach high, for stars lie hidden in your soul.
Dream deep, for every dream precedes the goal.
~ Pamela Vaull Starr, Poet, Artist, & Writer

CORE Example

YOUR ONE YEAR GOALS
Age: 18   Year: 2015

SUBJECT	GOALS	WHY	HOW	WHEN (Timeframe)
Education / Personal Development	Enroll in college / BS degree	Land a high paying professional job.	Study hard to maintain good grades. Get 3.5 GPA.	Freshman year
Career	PT night manager	Need money to help pay for college & expenses.	Work nights and weekends while in college.	20 hours per week.
Relationship	Date different people	Find out my likes & dislikes in people.	Join clubs & sports. Meet people in same major.	Date on weekends.
Family	Monthly visits	Important to have them always in my life.	Ongoing contact and quality time while visiting.	Visit at least monthly.
Location	Move into college dorm	Required for out of state students.	Request same type of roommates & find suitemates for next year.	College years
Mentors Role Models	Business & spiritual mentors & role models	For faster progress in career & spiritual growth.	Seek out & ask exceptional people for their mentorship. Research role models	Each year of the ten year plan.
Financial	Get 4 year college loan	To pay for college expenses.	Apply for loan & keep part time job for income.	Qualify each year for loan.
Vacation	Take a vacation to Florida with friends	Always wanted to see Florida but never could.	Save $100 each month until I have enough for this trip. Drive with friends.	Freshman spring break.

CORE Worksheet

YOUR ONE YEAR GOALS

Age: **Year:**

SUBJECT	GOALS	WHY	HOW	WHEN (Timeframe)

Setting and Balancing Priorities Towards Success

The key is not to prioritize what's on your schedule, but to schedule your priorities.
~ Stephen Covey, Author, Businessman, & Keynote Speaker

What are your priorities in life? How do you manage to strive for your short and long-term goals you established and pay attention to other priorities? We are discussing the art of balancing priorities as you strive for your objectives in life. It is unwise to be obsessed with achieving your goals and neglecting the other important people and events in your life. Hence, priorities will keep you balanced.

The definition of "priority" in the Merriam-Webster dictionary is; *"something that is more important than other things and that needs to be done or dealt with first; the things that someone cares about and thinks are important; the condition of being more important than something or someone else and therefore coming or being dealt with first."*

With that, it is important to recognize those people and things that you consider to be the most important in your life and how they translate into your goals. The trick is to find the balance in dealing with your priorities of what's happening in the present while keeping an eye on your future goals and trying to attain them.

Managing your time effectively is an important element in all of this. We talked about setting long-term goals and then coming up with some short-term goals to get you there. To take this one step further, you can break activities down into monthly, weekly or daily objectives. In doing so, you can focus on the right priorities while still paying attention to all other priorities. For example, as an author, I needed to review my book before sending it to print. Although my desire was to have it reviewed in its entirety by midweek, I realized that would be too overwhelming and limited time for other priorities. Instead, I scheduled four hours each day to proof three steps at a time. By repeating this process day after day the entire book was reviewed by the following Saturday. Attacked in this way, goals are not so hard to reach. Each time I met a daily objective, I felt in control over this book priority and balancing all other priorities. It built up confidence in the process and intensified commitment to keep forging ahead.

Your personal priorities can be managed systematically in a number of ways. By writing down your monthly, weekly, and daily priorities you keep a better balance in your life. You will also begin to see how these priorities relate to your one-year goals, which in turn get you closer to achieving your ten-year plan.

Establishing Priorities

1. Priorities should reflect what activities or tasks you want to accomplish within the time frame identified.

2. They can be individual priorities or family/group activities.

3. Your priorities need to be specific and measureable, same as goals.

4. If the priority includes others, then communication of the task/activity needs to be agreed upon by those involved.

5. Update daily, weekly and monthly activities.

6. You can add, delete, or revise your priority list at any time.

Depending on your relationships in life, one approach to managing priorities is holding family or group meetings. Our family would hold a weekly meeting to talk about what our schedules would be like during the upcoming week. We felt it was well worth 60 minutes of our time each week to discuss who is doing what, where they will be doing it and when. By disciplining ourselves to sit down and think through the events and concerns over the next week, we accomplish more in synch as a family unit. Sometimes our lives are so hectic that we miss a week or two, and that's when our priorities most often become muddled.

TAKEAWAYS: Priorities

- Setting daily, weekly, monthly priorities with others in relationships around you is important.

- Managing your time effectively will help you balance your focus on goals and taking care of other areas of your life.

- Setting personal priorities & writing them down gives you a good idea of how these priorities relate to your short & long-term goals.

- Enjoy the journey as you strive for your goals.

The key is not to prioritize what's on your schedule, but to schedule your priorities.
~ Stephen Covey, Author, Businessman, & Keynote Speaker

Exercise #3D: Priorities by Month, Week and Day

Objective:
- Identify your priorities needed to fulfill your short term goals.

Steps:
- There are numerous methods of recording your priorities and everyone will determine what suits them best. You can use individual worksheets for your different types of priorities (daily, weekly, or monthly) or you could use one worksheet that combines all of your priorities. We have chosen to use one worksheet combining all priorities as an example.

- Write down the subjects that require attention. These subjects should be linked to the subjects in your short term goals

- Determine time frame, daily, weekly, monthly.

- Indicate the Priority ranking from A1 (highest) – C1 (lowest).

- Identify what tasks or activities are required to complete priority

Success is having a flair for the thing that you are doing; knowing that is not enough
—you have got to have hard work and certain sense of purpose.
~ Margaret Thatcher, Former Prime Minister of Great Britain

EXAMPLE OF PRIORITY WORKSHEET / MONTHLY, WEEKLY, DAILY

Priority ABC	Timeframe	Priority by Subject	Activity / How
A1	Daily	Education/College	Complete application to enroll into college and submit.
A2	Daily	Financial/College	Apply for 4 year college loan.
A3	Daily	Career/PT Work	Work 6-9 pm tonight.
B1	Weekly	Relationship/Dating	Join college club to meet different people this weekend.
B2	Weekly	Mentor/College	Call & visit college professor as potential mentor.
B3	Weekly	Career/Internship	Write letters to financial institutions asking to be involved in internships.
C1	Monthly	Financial/College	Save $300 for college fund.
C2	Monthly	Financial/Vacation	Save $100 for trip to Florida with friends.
C3	Monthly	Family/Visits	Schedule third weekend to drive home to visit family.

PRIORITY WORKSHEET / MONTHLY, WEEKLY, DAILY

Priority ABC	Timeframe	Priority by Subject	Activity / How

www.achievingsuccesscenter.com

Enjoy the Journey

As important as your goals for success are, even more important is the journey you take to reach success. Work and strive to reach your goals, but don't obsess or stress over them. Reach your goals with positive attitudes and balanced lives. After all, the moment in time when you get to your goals is short in comparison to the time you spend traveling on the path to reach them. This is why you want to enjoy the time it takes to reach your goals and make the journey more important than any particular goal.

In my life, I had not done a very good job of making the journey more important than the goal. In fact, my goals were the most important to reach at any cost in relationship to the journey. This has made the journey for the loved ones in my life stressed and challenging at times. Furthermore, they have told me that they cannot keep pace with me nor interested in doing so. Too often, I ignored their expressions of frustration and kept running forward, despite their objections. Not only was this difficult for the others around me, but I found out soon that I too could not keep the pace I set at times. The penalty I paid turned out to be the decline in my health which resulted in two back surgeries to correct my aggressive, non-stop flight to success. How wrong I was to think and behave this way and not truly enjoy the journey.

The point is, you want to avoid just the passion of fulfilling goals and replace this with the passion of enjoying the journey along the way to reaching your goals.

On a recent business trip I met a man who shared his belief on how goals and the journey should come together. He stated that the journey ought to be like walking on a *"people mover"* (known as the "moving walkway") in the airport. You walk at an enjoyable pace on the people mover, moving quickly past the crowd. The people mover represents a journey with defined goals in which the journey can be easier and more enjoyable. Whereas the crowd represent people without defined goals, taking them much longer to complete their journey.

There are many people in the world who have a difficult time enjoying the journey. If you are one of these people, you most likely want to know how to enjoy the journey versus what you are doing now. Although there are no magic answers, you probably need to make certain adjustments in your present lifestyle. What are some of the changes you can consider?

Here are a few suggestions:
- "Just Say No" to additional activities that don't help you achieve your goals or do not provide enjoyment to your journey.

- Simplify your life by removing habits, activities, and events that add stress to your journey and are not necessary.

- Clearly state in advance what priorities are more important than others. This reduces the stress and frustration of deciding what priorities fit into your journey.

- Communicate to others your desired approach of traveling on your life journey.

- You need to make a conscious effort to live more in the present moment and enjoy what is happening around you.

Creating a Personal Mission Statement

This next exercise completes the concept of "where are you going?" established as the theme of this step. The value of completing a personal mission statement is defining who you want to be and how you want to live your life.

Mission statements are documents that define the purpose, goals and principles of individuals, families, companies, organizations, governments, etc. It is considered the "Declaration of your Personal Doctrine." For the teaching purposes of this book, we will focus on your personal mission statement.

A personal mission statement reflects your individual goals, philosophies, core values and operating principles of life. It includes the purpose of your life and gives you a sense of direction and strategy of how to live. There isn't one blanket formula for any mission statement, as the variables will reflect the uniqueness of each individual. Here are guidelines to consider using along with core components that when included, create a strong mission statement.

GUIDELINES:

1. A personal mission statement can be as brief as a few sentences or as lengthy as you choose.
2. A personal mission statement is your statement of purpose(s) =or objective(s) for the focus of the mission statement.
   - Specific Purposes in life or life in general
   - Career or activities
   - Relationships or partnerships
   - Spiritual life or faith life
3. You can include:
   - Commitment statements
   - Behavior expectations
   - Personal values
   - Strategies for execution of purpose/objectives.
   - Any of your own ideas as this is your individualized mission statement
4. Conclusion statement

COMPONENTS:

1. **Purpose/Objective:** This statement is the driving force of the mission and should be clear and concise. It is the purpose/objective for you as an individual. If the mission statement is all-inclusive, such as success with all personal aspects of your life, than your purpose/objective will need to be more complex in nature. The purpose/objective would reflect wide-ranging goals. However, if the mission statement is specific in nature, such as related only to your spiritual well-being, than your purpose/objective would be more definitive in terms of spiritual or faith objectives.

2. **How:** It should describe what measures you will take to accomplish the purpose/objective. This can be simple or as strategic as you choose.

3. **Roles:** Identify your roles or responsibilities as they relate to your purpose/objective. An example could be your combined roles as a mother, wife, and daughter. Your goals and responsibilities for each of these roles need to be defined. A second example would be, if you are focusing on career oriented mission statement, your roles may include manager, subordinate, and co-worker. Each of these roles would require a statement.

4. **When:** Define specific time periods when you will be focused on your purpose/objective per each of these identified roles and how it may influence your mindset and behavior.

5. **Manner:** These could be affirmations of how you behave based on your purpose/objectives. These affirmations should reflect acceptable practices, policies or expectations.

6. **Summary:** This should summarize the desired end result of your mission purpose/objective.

Developing a mission statement takes effort and reflection. The more precise and complete, the more effective it will be in delivering your desired total life balance. It would be a strong recommendation that you revisit your mission statement at least annually or revise it as often as your purpose/objective changes or needs refinement.

Dennis' Personal Mission Example:

My first orientation to writing personal mission statements came during a two-day seminar with Stephen Covey, author of the book *First Things First*, co-chairman of the Franklin Covey Company and a widely-respected authority on leadership skills. These are the components used to complete this process.

1. **Purpose/Objective:** My first step was to identify the components, those listed above, which were influenced by the teachings of Stephen Covey. Creating the *"purpose/objective"* required a great deal of reflection as I wanted it to be all-inclusive yet focused on my passion for sharing new learnings with others. Recognizing that helping others would have to include sharing of knowledge to some degree, my purpose was written as such, "Use the knowledge that has been granted to me through academics, spiritual teachings and alternative learnings to better the lives of my family, friends, and individuals who desire assistance in achieving success in their lives." This would be considered a broad yet concise objective that is far reaching in its results.

2. **How:** Now with the purpose clarified, I needed to determine *"how"* this broad objective would be achieved. In order for me to help others achieve success through sharing knowledge and learnings, it would require a commitment on my part to always be a student, learning beyond my current understandings. This strive for continuous learnings would necessitate my own personal odysseys of learnings. The odyssey of learning involves seeking out scholarly instructors in areas of education, spiritual teachings, finances, business, geopolitical, universal wisdom and more. Attending seminars, workshops, in-services, classes, lectures and other learning situations to develop new knowledge would be "how" I fulfill the purpose of my learnings. The second part of the "how," which is to help others achieve their success in life, also needed to be addressed. Based on the different roles in my life, my "how" will vary. I would help my children as I raised them and offer assistance and information to my extended family whenever possible. Those outside my family unit, I would provide guidance in the workplace, seminars to spread the knowledge of achieving success, and providing written materials through my books and seminars that would help them achieve success in their lives.

3. **Roles:** Once I understood how I would share my knowledge of achieving success, it was important to define my various *"roles"* with others and prioritize them. First and foremost is my role as a husband and father. As a husband, I want to provide my wife with emotional support as well as to assist in the day-to-day activities of our life together. Her personal happiness is of utmost importance not only to herself but to our entire family. As a father I want to provide a great deal to my children, but what takes the lead here is to be a good role model and mentor—one who gives unconditional love and provides them with the tools to succeed in life.

Next, there is my role as a business owner, boss and peer in the workplace. My obligation here is to insure successful business results in an environment where everyone involved can experience personal and professional growth. Many people are depending on me in this role for their own well-being and their families. It is important that everyone in the company benefits from my assistance with achieving the company goals and success.

And lastly, I strive to make a difference in the lives of those who I have the opportunity to help, including extended family members and the world's less fortunate. The seminars, and including this book, are designed to assist others outside of my circle of family, friends and acquaintances, and their quest for achieving success.

4. **When:** It seems clear that the *"when"* component of this mission statement overlaps with the role component. As described in the roles, I will use every opportunity while raising my children and being happily married to my wife, to assist in all ways of their growth and development. Always with the goal of being successful in our relationships and life. Almost daily, the workplace will provide me with the opportunities to guide, instruct and present in-services that will offer growth for all those within my

reach. For those outside of my personal reach, I would hold success seminars and circulate my book to provide them with knowledge and learnings that will help them achieve their fullest potential for success.

5. **Manner:** How you see yourself and the "*manner*" in which you present yourself to people are factors not to be overlooked when you write your personal mission statement. After all, you can only effect change if you are received well by those you are trying to help. Your behavior, your attitude and your manner will influence others acceptance of your assistance. For instance, I outlined the following 6 points in my personal mission statement as the manner in which I would try to conduct myself throughout my lifetime.

- I will invariably keep my promises and be honest.
- I will use positive energy in my life to help people, and I will look for the "good" in people and situations.
- I will keep a balance between having courage to address situations that are uncomfortable while being considerate of the other's needs who are involved in the issue being addressed.
- I will always share my knowledge with others.
- I will act responsibly in all areas of my life.
- I will be polite and treat people as I wish to be treated.

6. **Summary:** The "*summary*" should be the concluding statement that is developed based on the other components. In context of my personal mission statement, the following is the summary I wrote, "In reaching my purpose of assisting others through the sharing of my knowledge and learnings, I will be remembered for providing guidance, knowledge, and mentorship whenever needed to all those within my circle of family, friends, acquaintances and others. My success seminars, books and workbooks provided learnings and methodologies that improved the lives of others.

The most important thing to me is that I leave behind no regrets of past deeds or actions, and that I did not fail to act when necessary. I also hope that, with the example I set, those people who are close to me will have gleaned some worthy principles to live by."

Exercise #3E: Personal Mission Statement

Objective:
- To create a personal mission statement that reflects your individual goals, philosophies, core values and operating principles of life.

Steps:
- **Purpose:** Formulate the purpose/objective in your life that you will be developing the mission statement around. Be concise. This could be an objective that is broad in scope or specific in nature. What are the main principles in your life by which you want to live? Write them down.
- **How:** Explain how you intend to reach the documented purpose or objective.
- **Roles:** Identify the different roles that may be involved while executing this purpose and their relevance to you.
- **When:** Determine when you will be providing the activity, actions, or follow though needed to achieve objective(s).
- **Manner:** Affirmations of your behavior, performance, or actions while fulfilling the purpose is important to document.
- **Summary:** This should summarize the desired end result of your mission purpose/objective.

EXAMPLE: PERSONAL MISSION STATEMENT

PURPOSE: To use the time, talent, health, knowledge and energy given to me by God to help better the world for persons and relationships in my sphere of influence.

HOW: I will accomplish this by recognizing the opportunities to teach, to give guidance, to listen, to understand and to help persons when I am in my various roles.

ROLE: These major roles, in order of priorities are: husband, father, boss/peer, business owner, member of extended family and friend of the world's helpless and desperate.

WHEN: First, take care of my needs; mental, physical, emotional and spiritual – which will help strengthen and insure my availability. Next, pre-plan and when possible, help those in my various roles. Do this in a balanced approach, without excess in any direction.

MANNER:
I will always keep my promises and be honest.
I will always look at the "best" in situations and use positive energy to help.
I will keep a balance between courage and consideration.
I will always share whatever possible.
I will always take care of my responsibilities.
I will always be polite and treat people as I would want to be treated.

SUMMARY: When I die, I will leave behind no regrets of past deeds, and actions or failure to act when needed.
When death comes, I will leave no baggage, instead I will leave behind examples of the good principles to live on.
I will look forward to my new adventure with excitement and positive attitude.

PERSONAL MISSION STATEMENT

PURPOSE:	
HOW:	
ROLE:	
WHEN:	
MANNER:	
SUMMARY:	

STEP 4

Attitude / Gratitude / Disciplines
"Daily Success Tools"

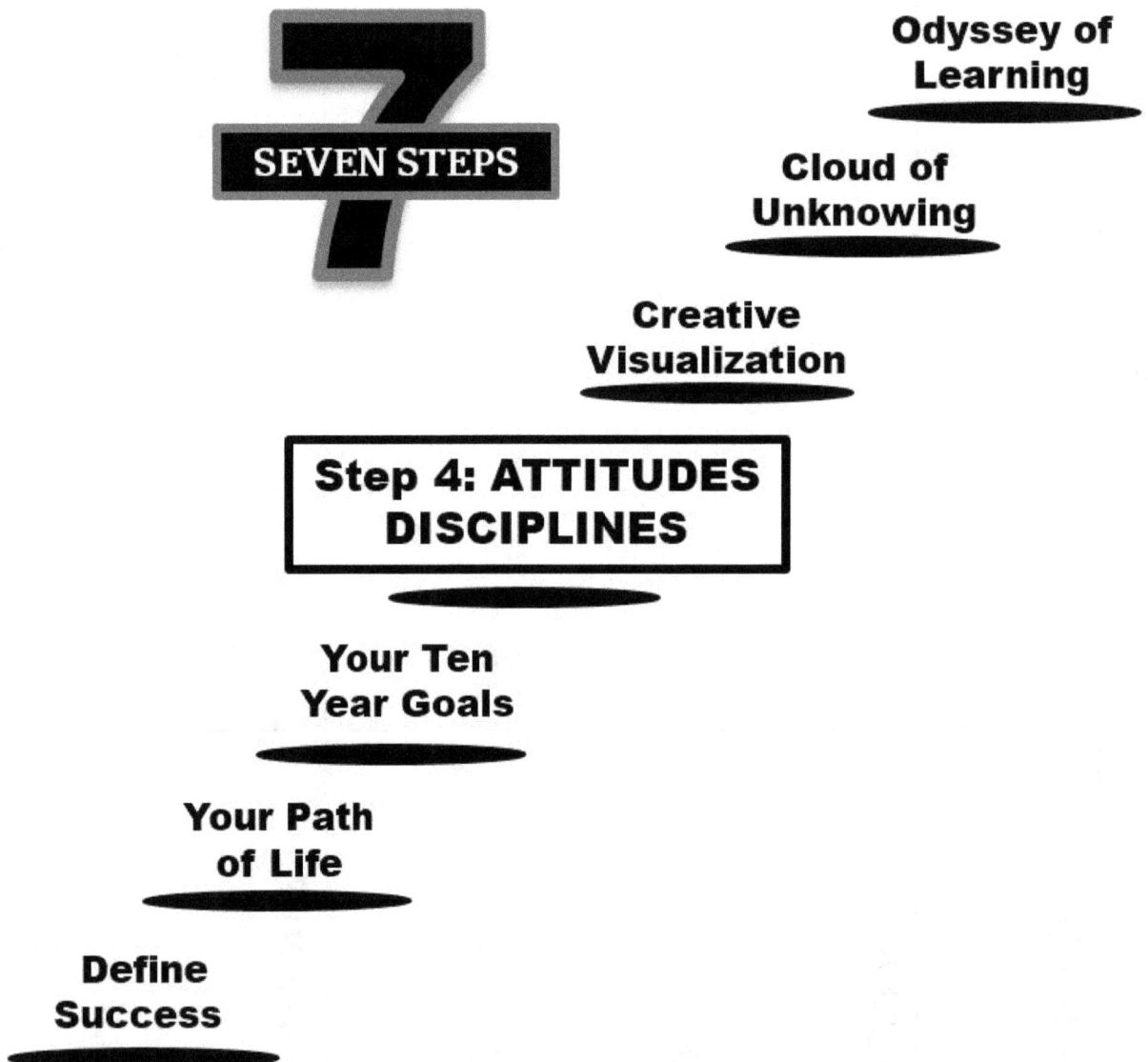

SEVEN STEPS (7)

Odyssey of Learning

Cloud of Unknowing

Creative Visualization

Step 4: ATTITUDES DISCIPLINES

Your Ten Year Goals

Your Path of Life

Define Success

If you change the way you look at things, the things you look at change.
~ Dr. Wayne Dyer, Author & Motivational Speaker

In this step, we will build upon the importance of attitudes, expressing gratitude, and disciplines. These are the daily success tools that are required to deliver your goals outlined in Step 3. We will share these three success tool and how to incorporate them into your life. However first, you will learn to recognize the differences between inconveniences and problems and the importance of adopting the right attitude when dealing with life's barriers.

One's path to success is not always smooth but the attitude you adopt can influence the dips in your life path. There will undoubtedly be barriers. How you react when things don't go the way you planned is significant? Take a look at your past reactions to life's challenges as reflected in your path of life you completed in Step 2. It may give you some insight into how to handle barriers in the future.

When you are confronted with a barrier in life, your challenge is to work around it. Do not allow it to become a deterrent in your life. There are many people who have overcome obstacles in their lives and gone on to greatness. Franklin Delano Roosevelt is a good example. At the age of thirty-nine he contracted polio and spent most of his life in a wheelchair, but that didn't stop him from becoming one of the greatest leaders of our nation. He was elected president of the United States four times.

In his mid-forties, music composer Ludwig van Beethoven became completely deaf, yet he wrote some of his finest music after his unfortunate loss of hearing.

Physical limitations are an obvious illustration of "life's not fair." What about losing a loved one, getting fired from your job, losing your home in a flood or fire, and other economic injustices? These are a few major setbacks that happen to people more often than you'd perhaps like to think about. You need to acknowledge that these things *do* happen—that life's not always fair.

Many people ask me why is "life not fair." The expression, "life's not fair" is not an external factor; it's an internal perception within people. Individuals create this perception within themselves whereby they experience the feeling of "life's not fair."

I'll give you a hypothetical example. Let's look at two different people and their situations. Take a gentleman who worked hard all of his life and accumulated millions of dollars by the age of forty. However, at age thirty-five, he developed degenerative disc problems in his back and, by age forty, he could hardly move around free of pain. He might view life as not being fair because he worked so hard for so long to achieve enough wealth to enjoy his life, yet his health prevented him from doing so. Is "life not fair" because everyone does not have the same good health?

Take a second young man who is perfectly healthy and played sports all the time. He did not finish high school so he was unable to get a good job which hindered his ability to get ahead financially. He could not afford to buy equipment or clothing for his sporting needs, so he couldn't travel with the team due to lack of financial resources. Is "life not fair" because everyone does not have the same amount of money?

So what is worse, having poor health yet lots of money or having no money but excellent health? The point is the perception that "life's not fair" is an internal perception and not an external factor. And that's good news, because if it is internal, **you** have the ability to mentally overcome this influence that you've produced by adjusting your mental attitude.

How? By accepting what you can do to overcome this so-called unfairness. What can you do to get past it and move on? I acknowledge that it's not always easy. The first step, however, is to adopt a positive attitude and forget about life not being fair. Then using a positive attitude, determine if life's deterrents are inconveniences or problems.

TESTIMONIAL

Salvatore A. Bonfante, Human Resources Manager, Lactalis American Group

"We needed to solve the problem of "Problem Solving". In the manufacturing environment, over time, problems repeat themselves. Employee's continue to turnover, so, when the problem comes up, and the new people are seeing it for the first time, the approaches to solving problems were all over the board.

When we interviewed Dennis for the job, he was very detailed, and had a very strong grasp of his material. His resume and client list was impressive. We could tell that he would be able to reach our employees due to his approach.

Dennis was able to have our employees first examine themselves and determine the types of thinkers they were. He introduced to them six different ways of thinking. The approach helped the employee to understand how they themselves thought. This enabled them to see also other ways of thinking and how to best approach the problem using a mix of all ideas.

It was a very good experience; the employees need to be open minded to accept change.

I would recommend this seminar to others because we need forward thinkers as time goes on. If you stand pat, your company will not realize its full potential in their number one resource...its people!"

Inconveniences vs. Problems

Some of the problems you think you have may only be inconveniences. What is the difference between inconveniences versus problems?

An inconvenience is a temporary disruption of your journey to reaching your long-term goals. These inconveniences might require additional time and resources for you to overcome, but you can overcome them somewhat easily and eventually achieve your long-term goals.

An inconvenience could be an auto accident in which your car is totaled but you remain unharmed. In this instance, you would need to spend some time and money filling out accident reports, insurance claims, renting a temporary car, looking at new cars, and waiting for a check from the insurance company to buy the new car. Most people would agree, this is still considered an inconvenience, not a problem.

A problem, on the other hand, is a serious disruption of your journey to reaching your long-term goals. Problems require large amounts of additional time, more financial resources, and a shifting of the focus you originally had on reaching your long-term goals. This necessary shift in focus may cause a significant or permanent delay in achieving your long-term goals.

Such a problem might be an auto accident where you total your car, lose the use of a limb, and tragically lose a loved one. Now this is a problem. This problem includes all the previously mentioned inconveniences, and in addition, you suffer the grief of losing your loved one, reestablishing your life without that person, and recovering from your own injuries that require hospitalization and prolonged rehabilitation. You have also experienced a loss of work, which means loss of income as well. These conditions will take your focus off your long-term goals, and rightfully so. At this point, you need to acknowledge that you have a problem. In doing so, you can at some point address a game plan to get past your problem and eventually refocus on new or adjusted long-term goals.

Many people treat inconveniences as if they are big problems, and they give them too much attention, causing their focus to be shifted from long-term goals to other insignificant events. It's really important to consciously stop and recognize the difference between an inconvenience and a problem.

Most inconveniences and many problems can be fixed. You can jump the hurdles, break through barriers, and make your way through a maze of stumbling blocks to correct the situation. Remember, identify your inconveniences versus your problems, and then figure out how much time, resources, and focus is required to manage them.

The purpose of this exercise is to help you change your mind set about what challenges you face in life.

I have learnt that success is to be measured not so much by the position that one has reached in life as by the obstacles which he has overcome while trying to succeed.
~ Booker T. Washington, Educator, Author, & Orator

Exercise #4A: Inconveniences versus Problems

Objective:
- To determine if the barriers in your life are inconveniences or problems.

Steps:
- Use the form below and list some of the barriers you are presently challenged with in your life.

- Take an objective look at these barriers and determine if they are inconveniences or problems. in the appropriate answer in the column on the right.

EXAMPLE: Inconveniences versus Problems

Life's Barriers	Inconvenience or Problem
Flat tire on thruway – rush hour	Inconvenience
Car collision – one dead, two hurt	Problem
Failed math – lost scholarship	Inconvenience
Lost job to downsizing	Problem
Got fired and no unemployment	Problem
Sunburn – in pain with blisters	Inconvenience
Skin cancer	Problem
Unexpected bill	Inconvenience
Foreclosure on house	Problem
Divorce	Problem

Inconveniences versus Problems

Inconvenience or Problem									
Life's Barriers									

Positive Attitude / Overcoming Barriers

The first of the three daily success tools is a positive attitude to overcome life's barriers. Now we will focus on sharing with you how to create new attitudes and behaviors in your life to achieve your goals and dreams.

If you believe the barriers you face are inordinately big and insurmountable, then you won't have much chance of overcoming them. If you focus on a barrier too much it tends to become magnified. When you're too close to a dilemma, it's often difficult to see a solution for it. It's like viewing a pointillist (made up of tiny dots) painting from a few inches away. There is no representational form. All you see are tiny dots of color until you step back and they blend together to form a discernible image. Sometimes you need to step back from the problem and stop dwelling on it in order for the answer to come.

Many people think they can solve their difficulties by changing their circumstances. But "circumstances are always neutral" says Richard Carlson, author of *"You Can Be Happy No Matter What."* It's the way you view your circumstances that matters, and the way you view them is often determined by your attitude at the time. In fact, changing your attitude is often the key, not your circumstance.

Carlson points out that "our view of individual circumstances will always change with our ever-changing attitude and feeling level. So, while there are times when working toward positive change is appropriate, we need not be stuck with change as the only possible answer."

Carlson uses the example that "almost everyone will go through periods of time when they feel they 'don't like what they do.' Many people fail to notice, however, that, most of the time, they like what they do. Because they trust what they feel in a lower state of mind, they jump from one job to another thinking that something else might bring them greater satisfaction. But in a low mood, this same person will not like his new career either. The same logic applies to other life situations as well."

I previously suggested that you not force any big life decisions when you're feeling at a low point emotionally or during a low dip along your path in life.

Keeping a positive attitude becomes second nature once you face challenges as inconveniences. So the next time you face life's barriers, approach them with a positive attitude and you will overcome both inconveniences and problems.

Very often we are our own worst enemy as we foolishly build stumbling blocks on the path that leads to success and happiness.
~ Louis Binstock Spiritual Advisor & Counselor

Attitude is Everything

How you manage your attitudes is key to dealing with your individual inconveniences and problems, as well as company-wide problems. I did not coin the phrase "attitude is everything," but I have shared it with many friends, family members, and clients.

One client of mine was responsible for a supermarket chain in South Africa. The chief executive within the organization was full of vision, leadership, and positive attitude. Being recently promoted, he faced the challenge of getting an entire organization to develop a positive attitude in order to tackle the many problems the company faced.

On one of my client visits to South Africa, I gave a presentation using positive attitudes for problem-solving and how the concept of "Attitude is Everything" is key to changing the company's cultural environment. Then I gave him a small gift for his hospitality. It was a hat bearing the inscription, "Attitude is Everything." He was so impressed with the concept that he used "Attitude is Everything" for the theme of the general managers meeting the following month. He even had the slogan inscribed on the company's newsletter (shown below). A positive attitude can be a very powerful tool in overcoming your inconveniences and problems.

Executive Bulletin

MAY 1996   GENERAL MANAGERS' MEETING SPECIAL   Pick n Pay 2000

Attitude is everything!

THE theme of the recent General Managers' Meeting held in Cape Town was "Attitude is Everything"! Held to discuss the '96 financial year-end results and make plans for the '97 financial year, it was the first to be held since our restructure. As you will have heard by now, the results show that our new revitalised "Pick 'n Pay 2000" is already reaping a good harvest for us because we have made a great turnaround, with better results than even the financial experts predicted. The assembled general managers heard chairman Raymond Ackerman, retail MD Sean Summers and group enterprises MD Gareth Ackerman tell them that there is a new feeling all around the company compared to that of a year ago. It is a positive feeling of enthusiasm that Pick 'n Pay is going back to the top, and of excitement as we enter new fields like the Theatre of Foods, centralised buying in general merchandise, centralised food distribution in the Transvaal, franchising, stationery stores, TranSwitch, and countries to the north of us. And our old "core" areas are not untouched! This positive attitude is showing itself everywhere in our stores because we can see the restructure is working; we are doing well and will be doing even better!

Adding to the get-up-and-go feeling of the meeting, several exciting announcements, awards and appointments were made which you can read about inside. Congratulations to these new appointees and award winners mentioned in this bulletin – we rejoice in their success with them and wish them well!

Surround Yourself with Positive People

Surrounding yourself with positive people breeds positive attitudes and outcomes. If you accept this, then the opposite would hold true. Negative people breeds negative attitudes and outcomes. This understanding leads into the next teaching, stay away from negative people.

I have had the pleasure of presenting my success seminars with a school in Buffalo, NY for over eleven years. One of the most powerful lesson learned by the students during the 2 day sessions was the concept of "Firing Your Friends." We shared with students not to get sucked into negative thinking by negative friends. The students were taken through these next steps.

- The students were asked to identify the type of people and their attitudes that surrounded them in their lives.
- They were then challenged to consider helping negative friends to change their negative attitudes into positive ones.
- The students were advised to fire them as their friends if they were unwilling to change. "Fire Your Negative Friends."
- It was encouraged that the students "surround themselves with people who have a positive attitude."

Remember, other people want to be surrounded by people with positive attitudes too. Are you one of those positive people? Think about it. Attitude is everything!

Using a Positive Attitude

Attitude is a component and influence in everything you do and say; in your thoughts, actions, and manner. Most people spend the majority of their lives working, therefore it stands to reason that attitudes play a significant role in the workplace.

In my first job as store manager at the supermarket chain, I had to deal with a person who had an incredibly negative attitude. Certainly you have met people like this too. Frustration overwhelmed me as I couldn't seem to get across to this individual that our method of doing business was changing within the company and he needed to change with it. As a solution, I wrote the following positive attitude statement on the wall of my office:

> *"The company is changing,*
> *You need to change with it.*
> *Negative attitudes won't stop it,*
> *Positive attitudes will make it easier.*
> *ADJUST!"*
> — Dennis J. Sobotka

Then I called this negative thinker into my office and told him that the company is bringing in these new shelf stocking processes and he would have to adapt to the changes. This message let him know that a negative attitude would not stop things from changing and that a positive attitude would actually make his life a whole lot easier. Adjust is the operative word here! It is true for everything, any kind of change that is taking place, anywhere. You must be flexible or you will continually come up against barriers in your life.

The sign remains on the wall in my office, many years later, as a reminder to myself, to keep adjusting to change with a positive attitude.

What is the difference between an obstacle and an opportunity? Our attitude toward it.
Every opportunity has a difficulty, and every difficulty has an opportunity.
~ J. Sidlow Baxter, Pastor, Theologian, & Author

Umbrella Management

A smart manager recognizes the power of positive attitudes. As the Director of hundreds of employees, I developed a management approach that centered on positive thinking. This is called "Umbrella Management." The umbrella management concept is: *A boss, who is responsible for others, holds up an umbrella over all of his employees to keep negative statements, attitudes, and situations away from raining down on his people. The boss controls the positive messages and attitudes that he wants his people to hear and focus on, while sheltering them from other negative attitudes.* People will eagerly work for this type of person and will be more productive employees.

A daily positive attitude is what my employees saw from me as their manager and consequently they were more positive and had greater productivity. You might ask, how can that exist in a corporate environment? Aren't people always walking into your office expressing negative attitudes about various situations? The answer is "yes," but that is where the concept of "umbrella management" comes into play. This working style crosses over into all aspects of life. Shelter those you are responsible for and breed a positive environment.

Attitudes: Umbrella Management

The boss controls the positive messages and attitudes while sheltering them negative attitudes.

Take Responsibility for Your Mistakes and Actions

If you think that being cynical or blaming others for your problems is a way to get past barriers in your life, you should think again. When you blame others, you are sharing a negative attitude. You take your hurdle and place it in someone else's playing field, hoping he or she will "take the fall" instead of you. Think about how often you blame others for things that have happened rather than acknowledging your mistakes and taking responsibility for your actions.

Cynicism has reached epidemic proportions in our society. People are cynical about government, economics, education, marriage and family. Those people with cynical attitudes are usually unwilling to take a good look at themselves, and they are least of all inclined to improve the very things they are cynical about. Cynicism is an indirect way of blaming others for your failure. When you can reproach yourself for your own blunders and accept your mistakes and imperfections, only then will you be able to overcome your difficulties with a positive attitude and move ahead.

When is the last time you took responsibility, raised your hand, and publicly acknowledged a mistake you made? "I made a mistake!" Think about it. Are you willing to acknowledge mistakes in front of your boss, your children, your spouse, your family members? Look around and ask yourself who you know that is not afraid to acknowledge his or her mistakes publicly?

Being principled, which means having integrity and taking responsibility for your actions, truly builds character. People recognize strong character in others and they respect them for it. They tend to want to be associated with individuals who have a healthy attitude and are willing to be accountable for their deeds and misdeeds. Employers gravitate toward hiring this type of person because they know in the end they're less likely to be dealing with a disgruntled employee. Stop blaming others!

Start Your Day Positive

A great piece I keep in my own personal packet of daily reflections is the following statement from an unknown author:

"Each and every morning when I wake up I will awaken with a very positive attitude. This positive attitude will be with me all day. I'll be aware of negative situations and negative people I come into contact with during the day, but as I become aware of them, which will be immediately, they will only stimulate and motivate me to be more positive. I'll be aware of any negative thought which happens to slip into my mind, but I'll immediately reject it as a useless thought."

~Unknown Author

This is a great statement because it represents the world you meet every day. I would teach this concept of having a positive attitude versus a negative attitude to my children when they were young. I used a skit in which I would act out this situation for them. In the skit, I started off by lying on the floor of our living room and pretending to be asleep. After a few snores, I woke up and expressed a positive attitude about something. Then, I pretended to meet people with negative attitudes. I conversed with these people about their negative state of affairs, and then responded to them with a positive twist.

Afterwards, each of my children joined in and we all played both the positive and negative roles. By practicing how to handle negative situations in a positive manner, it has helped my children to respond to negative situations.

To encourage my children to use this positive attitude, I would tell my children that a positive attitude is worth $10,000 dollars. I would use the piece of paper with the quote, "Each and every morning ..." as the motivator. They did not believe that reciting this positive affirmation quote each day would really transform into $10,000. However, the fact is, I did receive my first check for $10,000 for delivering business consulting services. I showed my children this check and reinforced the message I had been sharing with them. This reality of a $10,000 check impacted the credibility of the power of a positive attitude for my children. Using positive attitudes and behaviors, there can be big checks in your life too!

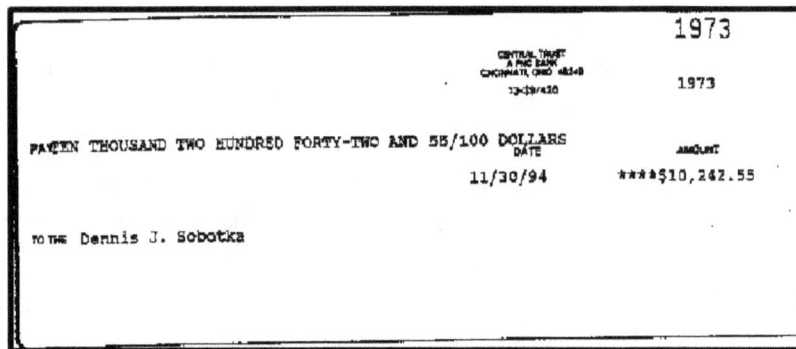

Positive attitudes and responses do not come easy, whereas negative attitudes and responses are quick to flow out. This applies to all people regardless of their age or position in life. We all need to practice positive attitudes and behaviors when handling negative individuals.

Thinking about your positive and negative attitudes, let us complete the next exercise which should enable you to accelerate your path to success.

Provide a haven from critical outside forces and upper management. Let your people know you have their back first and foremost, even when balancing the demands coming down from above.
~ Scott Mcdowell, Author

TAKEAWAYS: Attitudes

- Keep a positive attitude in your life. More than any other factor, it will help you jump the hurdles and get you further along your path to success.

- Acknowledge most of your problems as inconveniences and should be treated with less energy and focus. This will keep you focused and moving forward on your path to success.

- Take responsibility for your actions and acknowledge your mistakes. It takes some courage, but other people will admire you for it and it builds character, as well.

- Practicing daily positive affirmations increase the attraction of positive outcomes.

Exercise #4B: Manifesting Positive Attitudes

Objective:
- To increase your positive energy and live your life with a positive attitude. You need to clean up your past before you can build a positive future.

Steps:
- Acknowledge and document your current negative attitudes. Then write next to those negative attitudes the new positive attitudes you will incorporate into your life to replace the current negative ones. Do this for three to five significant attitude changes you wish to make.

- Determine when you blamed others and begin accepting personal responsibility for your behavior. Do this for three to five "blame" situations and correct your future behavior with positive energy.

EXAMPLE: Attitude and Blame

Negative: PRESENT Attitudes	Positive: NEW Attitudes
Assuming the worst in _people_.	Expect the best in people.
Assuming the worst _outcome_ in situations.	Expect the best outcome in situations.
Believing you are alone and unloved.	Realize there are people who care about you
Believing what will go wrong, does go wrong.	Acknowledge wrong & believe in positive solutions.
Talking _trash / gossip_ about others.	Be respectful and compliment others often.
Negative: Blaming Others	**Positive: Accepting**
Blaming my _spouse_ for my lateness.	I am the one always delayed.
Shifting blame to my _coworkers_.	Take responsibility for my mistakes.
Blaming my _parents_ for my failures.	Taking responsibility for my actions/results.
Siblings don't live up to my expectations.	Acknowledge siblings are unique & its OK.
Blaming "_They_" for my circumstances.	Accepting circumstances are neutral.

Attitude and Blame

Negative: PRESENT Attitudes	Positive: NEW Attitudes					Negative: Blaming Others	Positive: Accepting				

Positive Affirmations

An affirmation is a written statement which asserts that something exists or is true. Therefore, a **positive** affirmation is a written statement asserting a positive truth that you will follow. Consider creating a list of new positive affirmations you will say to yourself and/or to others as you go through the day.

Your statement should begin with "I will ..." and end with how you will think and/or behave relative to a subject or task that you are positively reinforcing. An example is when you awaken each morning you will start by professing something positive that you will adopt during the day. This can be a positive attitude, behavior or action.

An affirmation can be as simple as what you plan on saying each day when you greet coworkers, employees and bosses. Or as broad as "I am grateful for everything I have already received." You can address as many different subjects as you have in your life. This will help you to increase your positive energy ball and increase the law of attraction of positive activities that will occur in your life. Take time to write your personal list of positive affirmations that will help change your life and attract more positive energy into it.

EXAMPLE OF POSITIVE AFFIRMATIONS
I am grateful for all the blessings in my life.
I know today will turn out to be a great day.
I know everyday is getting better in my life.
I know what I visualize will happen in my life.
I will be pleasant and respectful to others.
I will think and pause before I speak.
I will be respectful and compliment others.
I will expect the best in people.
I will not be influenced by negative people.
I believe in myself to rise above new challenges.
I am responsible for my circumstances.
I will find positive solutions for all challenges today.
I will make good decisions by listening to my intuition.
I will make progress on completing my goals today.

POSITIVE AFFIRMATIONS

Gratitude is an Effective "Positive Energy" Attitude.

The second daily success tool discussed in this step is gratitude. As powerful as positive attitudes are, true gratitude is an equally powerful tool to achieve your goals and dreams.

Gratitude, as defined in the Oxford Dictionary, is "the quality of being thankful; readiness to show appreciation for and to return kindness." I consider gratitude one of the most effective expressions of positive attitudes. Adopting the expression of gratitude will generate positive energy in one's life and increases your ability to achieve your success. Gratitude is a powerful tool and should be included as a core principle when putting together your life success plan.

Gratitude attracts positive energy and positive outcomes. What does this mean? It is similar to the understanding of the "law of attraction." In a simplified explanation, the "law of attraction" refers to positive energies attracting positive outcomes and negative energies attracting negative outcomes. This attraction of energies is the concentration in the book "The Law of Attraction" by Jerry and Esther Hicks, and an integral part of "The Secret," by Rhonda Byrne. The power of gratitude holds the same positive energy as the power of attraction. The only difference is the approach the individual takes in leveraging positive energy. When an individual stops to acknowledge, to understand, and to finally embrace the law of attraction, one will appreciate the power of gratitude.

Expressing gratitude is not always easy nor does it come natural for some people. To create the positive energy flow through the expression of gratitude, it must be done sincerely. It should be your singular focus when expressing thanks, which then heightens the magnetic power of the law of attraction.

Now there are many different forms of showing gratitude and giving thanks in our lives. It will vary from individual to individual and usually will depend on your personality type. I would be remise not offering some examples no matter how elementary they might seem to some. Keep in mind, they don't all apply to everyone, and these are but a few of many ways to express or show gratitude.

Today people are less apt to pick up the phone and speak to others when we are looking to express ourselves. We seem to exhaust all other modes of communication first before breaking down and just calling someone. How long would it really take for you to call that individual to personally show your thanks and gratitude? What an impact that would have on someone's day, to receive such a positive call. This used to be the normal means of expressing thanks that most people would assume and practice.

Another expression of gratitude can be in a written form. It can be a personalized thank you note or letter, or an email showing appreciation, which are all acceptable forms of expressing thankfulness. In today's technological world, the younger generation would also include the art of texting as being an acceptable form. It isn't necessarily the type of written form used but rather the sincerity of showing gratitude that heightens the magnetic power of attraction.

One of the most common and powerful forms of expression is in the form of prayer. When speaking of praying it usually refers to expressing oneself to a higher being. Keeping within that context, the expressing of gratitude in prayer intensifies the thankfulness and positive energy toward that which you are thankful for. In many ways an individual could just use prayer as a form of expressing gratitude.

The next form of expressing gratitude is focused on my daily reflection of thankfulness. This tool is simple yet very effective and is called my *"gratitude list"*! You need to make a daily commitment to capture in writing moments of gratitude that occur throughout the day to reinforce them. The concept is to help an individual move away from a negative perception of their life and force them to write down three positive events that occur in which they express gratitude for each day. This written tool was adopted out of necessity when mentoring others who were engulfed in negative energy and spiraling downward. In order to understand why my gratitude list has become such a powerful tool for me and others, you need to understand a concept I call "two energy balls." This is based on my understanding of universal energy and the results manifested by individuals who have embraced this concept.

Each of us has two balls of energy within our body, one negative energy ball and one positive energy ball. Your success in life is influenced by which of these two balls of energy control your daily attitudes. If this is an accepted truth, than one would conclude having a large and ever present positive energy ball would be to our advantage. Therefore, when you allow your negative energy ball to exceed greater than your positive ball it becomes harder to find the positives in your life. The negativism seems to become unstoppable and that's when the saying holds true, "When one thing goes wrong, everything else seems to go wrong too." And that negative energy ball can grow to be so overwhelming that you become stifled in this warp of negativism reaching saturation in size compared to your positive energy ball.

How does one change this situation and help to reverse the energy flow and increase the size of the positive energy ball? A simple answer to this would be focusing on the positive situations in your life and stop dwelling on the negative. However, as simple as that sounds, it is not easy to do when you are wrapped up in negativism. Often individuals need outside assistance either from a caring person in their lives or a professional who can offer an objective and balanced direction. That is when a good mentor can help divert your attention away from your misguided attitudes and encourage you to embrace a greater percentage of positive attitudes.

Now that you have a better understanding of our energy balls, let's look at utilizing the gratitude list. Again, out of necessity a simple one-page sheet has been created in which I asked people who mentor to write down their three main positive activities or happenings for each day of the week. This simple exercise of writing down your three positive gratitude occurrences increases significantly the positive energy drawn in by the law of attraction. The positive ball of energy then starts to increase in size and the negative ball of energy starts to decrease. The initial goal is to change the direction of energy flow from negative to positive. From that point, the second goal is to get the positive energy ball to the same size as the negative ball, equally them out. Finally, the next goal is to exceed the negative energy ball and continue to expand the positive energy ball to as large as possible reducing the negative ball of energy as you go along.

The most amazing part of this exercise was as the facilitator, I would fill out my three positives for each day as an example and send it to the individuals I would be mentoring. These individuals were all stuck in their negative ball of energy which was spiraling out of control. My goal was for them to combat their negativism by recognizing all their positive happenings each day no matter how minuscule in comparison to others and get the positive energy ball back in motion. While this expression of daily gratitude made a significant impact in their lives and improved their positive energy flow, as their facilitator, I too experienced significant rewards. My daily gratitude list increased my positive energy ball and amazing things happened in my life beyond my normal anticipated routines. I continue to be impressed with the power of this simple but effective approach. Use this gratitude list tool for one month and then assess its effectiveness in your life.

An example of a basic 7-day gratitude worksheet to capture these positive experiences on a daily basis is below. A form is not required to use this exercise effectively. These three positive daily experiences can be written on a 3 x 5 notebook, into your cell phone or on a napkin, whatever works for you. Just do it!

Feeling gratitude and not expressing it is like wrapping a present and not giving it.
~William Arthur Ward, Writers of Inspirational Maxims

TAKEAWAYS: Gratitude

- Gratitude is a very effective expression of a positive attitude. It will generate an abundance of positive energy in your life which then manifests into achieving success.

- Practicing daily positive affirmations increase the attraction of positive outcomes.

WEEKLY GRATITUDE WORKSHEET

Day/Date ___	I am Very Thankful. Gratitude #1	I am Very Thankful. Gratitude #2	I am Very Thankful. Gratitude #3
Sunday			
Monday			
Tuesday			
Wednesday			
Thursday			
Friday			
Saturday			

WEEKLY GRATITUDE WORKSHEET

Day/Date _____	I am Very Thankful. Gratitude #1	I am Very Thankful. Gratitude #2	I am Very Thankful. Gratitude #3
Sunday			
Monday			
Tuesday			
Wednesday			
Thursday			
Friday			
Saturday			

DISCIPLINES

Discipline is the catalyst that pulls together everything we do, and without which we flounder helplessly, no matter how great our native ability or opportunities.
~Arthur Mitchell, Ballet Director & Choreographer

Disciplines and Their Influence on Achieving our Success.

This is the third daily success tool discussed in this step on how to achieve your goals and dreams. With appreciation of your new attitudes and gratitude, you now need to create new disciplines in your life.

The definition of discipline is "behavior in accord with rules of conduct; behavior and order maintained by training and control." Now for some people, this word discipline is associated with sacrifice, unpleasant tasks or unhappiness. However for many others this word is embraced and credited to their success due to their personal disciplines. For our purposes, disciplines will be considered positive catalysts in our life, providing us with missing components needed to achieve our success. We will use the term habits when referring to old habits that you identify in need of changing. Disciplines will be the new habits, those replacing the bad habits.

Using this daily success tool, you will focus on disciplines in relationship to achieving your definition of success as you outlined in Step 1. In order to understand what disciplines will be helpful, you need to work backwards by revisiting your personal mission statement and your ten year goals in Step 3. Now ask yourself this question, "What changes do I need to make in my life to reach these ambitious goals?" To do this, you need to identify your current bad habits? Refer back to your SWOT exercise in Step 3 where you listed your weaknesses and determine what bad habits are associated with these weaknesses. Decide what new disciplines you need to replace these bad habits.

The next step is to take this list of disciplines and methodically determine what you need to do to evoke these changes. It is important that you write down these new disciplines with as much detail as possible. For example, are they related to your eating habits or exercise routines or financial planning, etc.? Identify each potential change that is needed and convert it to a defined new discipline that you can embrace and incorporate into your life. These disciplines need to become your new habits that you integrate into your daily, weekly, and monthly lifestyle.

What lies in our power to do, lies in our power not to do.
~ Aristotle, Greek Philosopher

TAKEAWAYS: Disciplines

- Disciplines are necessary to achieving your goals.

- Recognize bad habits and commit to replacing them with new disciplines.

- Putting your Disciplines in writing intensifies your commitment to adopting them.

Exercise #4C: Disciplines

Exercise #4c consists of two worksheets, the first is to help you identify your old bad habits and create new disciplines to replace them. The second worksheet will assist you in developing new disciplines that will increase your success in life.

First Worksheet: BAD HABITS/NEW HABITS

Objective:
- Recognize your current bad habits and determine what changes are needed. Create a new and complete list of new disciplines that will assist you in reaching your mission statement and your ten year goals.

Steps:
- Start by listing at least five current bad habits identified in your SWOT exercise in Step 2 that work contrary to achieving your goals.

- Write down new positive disciplines that will replace your old habits. These new disciplines should be designed to achieve your success goals.

Second Worksheet: ADDITIONAL DAILY DISCIPLINES

Objective:
- Now that we have replaced bad habits, let's move on to create a list of additional new positive disciplines you will use as you go through the day. You will focus on improving your disciplines in many different areas of your life. This will help your productivity and efficiency in completing your monthly, weekly, and daily priorities to keep a better balance in your life as we discussed in Step 3.

Steps:
- Identify situations in your daily routine that need improvement.

- Create new disciplines that will improve these situations in your daily routine.

- Incorporate these new activities consistently for 30 days. After this time frame, they will become automatic as part of your lifestyle. Start by adding 5 to 10 new disciplines.

EXAMPLE: Creating Positive Disciplines

OLD BAD HABITS	NEW DISCIPLINES
Lack of exercise	Establish 3x week routine of exercise
Procrastinator	Act on decision-making
Late night TV – too tired in AM	Set deadline / prepare self for bed earlier
Lack of self control	Pause, count to 10 before speaking/acting
Consume too much beer/alcohol	Stop, agree to weekly limitations
Smoker	Stop, set timeframe to stop smoking
Sweet tooth	Limit sweets per day, per week
Anger management issues	Pause, think consequences before acting
Judgment of others	Stop before speaking unkindly of others
Spend too much time watching TV	Limit to 1 hour per night, read a book
Spend too much time on social internet	Limit time daily, walk away, focus on goals

Creating Positive Disciplines

NEW DISCIPLINES	OLD BAD HABITS

EXAMPLE: YOUR DAILY DISCIPLINES

Time	SUBJECT	DISCIPLINE	WHY	HOW
AM	Mind	Morning prayers / scripture readings	Nourish spiritual self	First activity out of bed
AM	Mind	Think positively each day	Attitude is everything	Ignore negative situations
AM	Mind	Read daily affirmations	To stay focused	Set time/location to read
AM	Health	5:00/6:00 AM start time	To achieve goals	Go to bed by 9 or 10:00 pm.
AM	Health	Healthy breakfast	Good nutrition for energy	Have correct food available
AM	Health	Exercise 20-30 mins	Gain energy, lose weight	Early gym attendance
Daily	Work	Deliver value everyday	Increase my value to the organization	Focus on good work performance
Daily	Work	Positive attitude with coworkers/boss	Encourage positive work place	Good attitude, helping nature
Daily	Work	Set daily work priorities	Productive work day	Focus on "A" priorities
PM	Personal	Spend time with family	Good balance in life	Nightly dinner together
PM	Personal	Acknowledge daily gratitude	Increase positive energy flow	Write 3 gratitude's daily
PM	Personal	Prepare for next work day/weekend	To maximize my time	Schedule activities, calls, and tasks
PM	Personal	Relax before bed	To sleep better free of stresses	Pray and read scripture

YOUR DAILY DISCIPLINES

Time	SUBJECT	DISCIPLINE	WHY	HOW

STEP 5

Creative Visualization

"Most Powerful Tool"

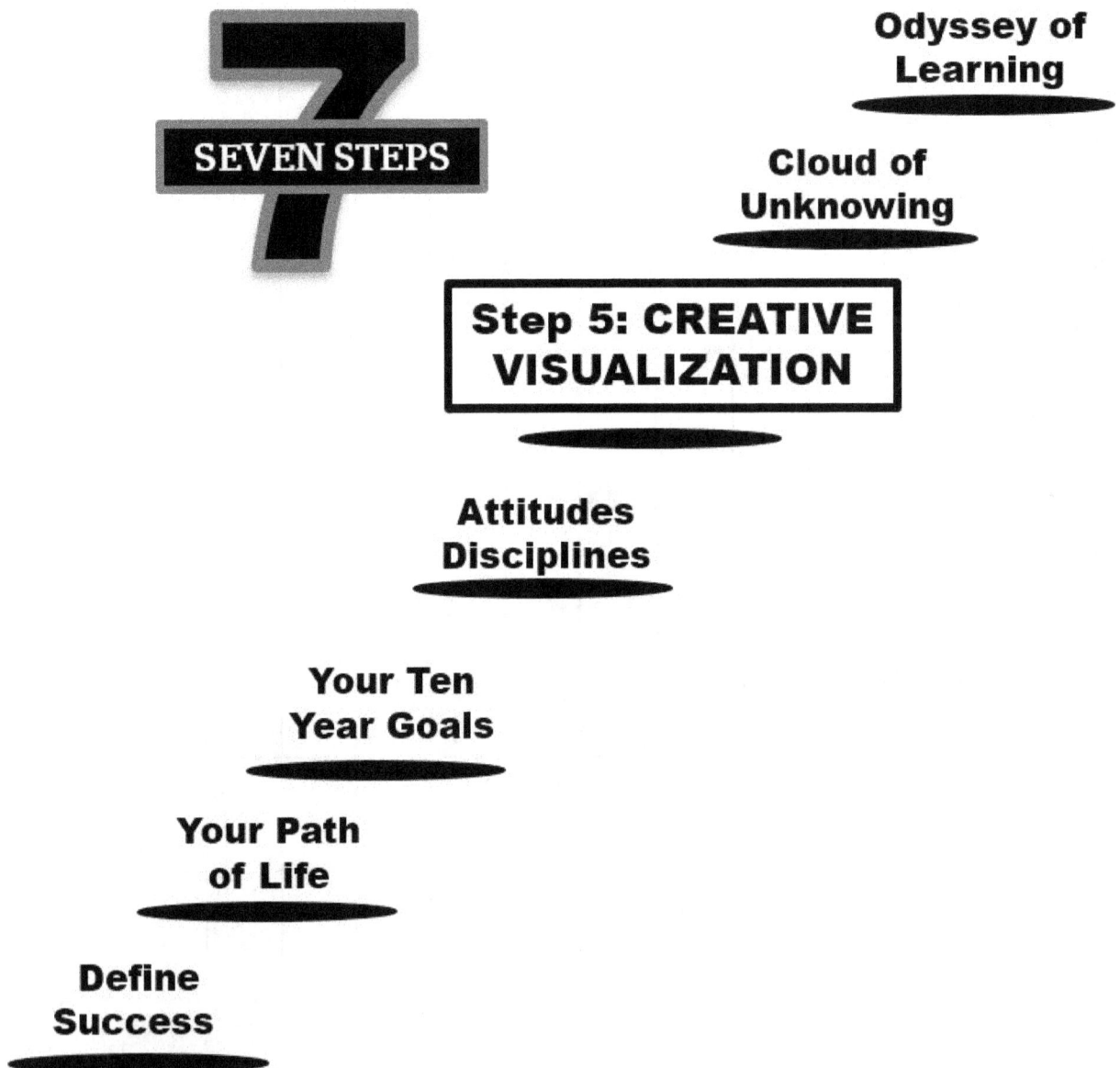

7 SEVEN STEPS

Odyssey of Learning

Cloud of Unknowing

Step 5: CREATIVE VISUALIZATION

Attitudes Disciplines

Your Ten Year Goals

Your Path of Life

Define Success

Imagination is the beginning of creation. You imagine what you desire,
you will what you imagine and at last you create what you will.
~ George Bernard Shaw, Nobel-Prize-Winning Playwright, Critic & Socialist

Visualization, as defined by Merriam Webster Dictionary, is *"the formation of mental visual images; the act or process of interpreting in visual terms or of putting into visible form."* Creative, as defined by Merriam Webster Dictionary, is *"having or showing an ability to make new things or think of new ideas."* Combining these two terms leads us to understand that the definition of "creative visualization" is the ability to visualize what you create in your mind and into physical reality.

Creative visualization is a tool used to achieve your goals through the process of converting your thoughts into energy and into everyday physical reality. This concept might be very new and unknown to many of our readers. To many it will seem unbelievable and not easily accepted nor embraced. Yet some of the most successful people in the world use this concept as one of their tools in achieving their success. We will share a few examples of these successful individuals and their success stories. We will discuss the power of creative visualization and how you can use this tool to your advantage.

The Principles of Creative Visualization are the following:
- Our **THOUGHTS** become our **WORDS**.
- Our **WORDS** become our **ENERGY**.
- Our **ENERGY** becomes our **PHYSICAL**.
- Our **PHYSICAL** becomes our **REALITY**!

This powerful tool is so underutilized because it is not taught in traditional schools. So I ask you, when reading this step, open your mind to embracing creative visualization and incorporating it into your daily activities. If you do so, you will find yourself among the many who have credited this technique to their success in life.

Your Mental Workshop

Imagine you're an artist holding a palette of colors in your hand. You are about to paint a picture you have envisioned in your mind. Slowly, you begin to paint in some lines on the canvas and fairly soon your painting begins to take shape. When you complete your artwork, the image you had visualized in your mind is before you.

Your mind is like a blank canvas. You have the ability to sit down and visualize in your mind's eye any scenario you desire. I'm sure that at one time or another you have thought about where you'd like to be on your next vacation. You may picture yourself on a great African safari or climbing Mount Everest. Or perhaps you pick up the travel section of your local newspaper and there's a two-page spread on the Caribbean islands. You see this image of a perfectly content person lying in a hammock being served an exotic beverage. You're there! That's you! You imagine yourself being there. The point is you have the ability to sit down and visualize it and imagine how you want it to happen.

Imagination . . . Its limits are only those of the mind itself.
~Rod Sterling, Screenwriter, TV Producer, & Narrator

Many times before a client presentation, I will take a few minutes to sit down, close my eyes, and visualize how I would like the presentation to proceed. This usually involves how I see myself interacting with the audience, how I might respond to a negative question by one of the listeners, and how I try to meet the eyes of those in attendance. I always end by visualizing the excitement the audience feels at the end of my presentation and their applause.

I shared this knowledge with my son and daughter when they were ages 4 and 6. I did so by taking them into the living room, where we got on the floor, closed our eyes, and turned out the lights. I introduced to them a concept to visualize, and then they would come up with their own visualization ideas. During this process, each of us talked about what we were visualizing. It worked perfectly, as we each visualized how we wanted to see different events take place in our lives. It was an effective teaching method and we called it our **mental workshop**.

Gina's Visualization Story

My daughter Gina was a soccer enthusiast. She played the sport since the age of five. One day before a game, when she was nine, she told me she wanted to score four goals, one for each person in our family. I was quite surprised by her announcement for two reasons. First, she had never scored more than one goal in any of her previous games, and, secondly, she had another commitment that day and would only be able to play three of the four quarters. At age 9 their soccer games were divided into quarters to give the youngsters more water breaks.

In her own words below, Gina describes what happened.

As we drove to the game, I sat next to my dad and I stated I would score one goal for each of my family members. My dad asked me to visualize how I was going to score these four goals, describing each one in detail. The drive took only about fifteen minutes, but by the time we reached the soccer field I was sure it was going to happen. Believe it or not, in the first quarter I scored two goals; the next quarter went by and I didn't score at all. But in the third quarter I scored another goal—I turned to my dad on the sidelines and put up three fingers. He smiled at me, even though there were only two minutes left before I had to leave the field. Before those two minutes were up, I shot the ball straight through the goalies' legs and scored again.

As my dad and I ran to the car, I asked him if this "stuff" (creative visualization) worked with other things. He said, "For Sure!"

Seeing the power of what her visualization brought in her soccer game, Gina continued to use this tool throughout her life. About a decade later, Gina had a dream to move to Boston for a summer adventure. Again she used her visualization techniques, and the rest is told in her "Three Boston Visualization" story.

"Three Boston Visualizations"

The following is a true story that took place in Boston where our family experienced three amazing visualizations on a grand scale.

1. Gina's Job in Boston: "VISUALIZED"

In January 2008, our daughter Gina's dream was to spend the summer in Boston working at an inner city school for 8 weeks. Gina was going to college to become a teacher and wanted to teach underprivileged students for experience.

Gina started in January applying and interviewing for a summer teaching program in Boston. In March she finally heard from the school that all summer school teacher's positions were filled however she would be placed on a waiting list. As time went on, there was still no job and Gina grew very impatient and frustrated. I told her to be patient and visualize herself in Boston teaching.

We had planned our Cape Cod vacation around Gina working in Boston just in case she got the job. Two weeks before we left for our vacation, and as Gina's frustration grew stronger, I placed 4 suitcases on one side of our room and placed 2 more suitcases on the other side. The 4 suitcases were for our Cape Cod vacation, while the other two were for Gina to pack clothes to live and work for 8 weeks in Boston. Gina packed them.

The day we were ready to leave Gina still had not heard from the school and had no job. Gina asked me, "Dad, what should we do?" As her father, I said to her "Load up the SUV with all 6 suitcases and believe you will get the job!" I reminded her to visualize it happening, and then we started our drive to Cape Cod. How many people would really add 2 large suitcases into a small size SUV, when there was so little room to begin with, for a job position that didn't exist?

We left for vacation not knowing about the job but two hours into our drive to Cape Cod, Gina received the long awaited phone call and was offered the job in Boston.

That was the first amazing visualization to manifest itself into reality, wow!

Now, that meant we had to change our course and drive directly to Boston to find living arrangements for Gina. We had only that evening to do so as our son would be arriving at the train station in Cape Cod the following day, expecting us to be there to pick him up. Talk about needing things to fall into place quickly.

2. Gina Finding an Apartment in Boston: "VISUALIZED"

By 5 PM we made it to Boston to find an apartment. We identified the safe areas for Gina to live in and then went on the internet checking for any apartments for rent. When all that didn't work, I started stopping people on the neighborhood street asking them if they knew anyone interested in a roommate.

Realizing I needed to make this happen, I stated out loud, "I like this street and want this for Gina. This is Gina's street!" I then visualized Gina living on this street for the eight weeks during her work experience.

The next two female students I ran into were the answer to our needs. What happened next was unbelievable - by believing, we found her an apartment to sublet with two nice female students on the very street we wanted.

Here lies the second amazing visualization to manifest itself into reality, wow!

After signing the lease agreement, we walked outside and just two doors down from her apartment building we found written in the cement sidewalk "GINA", all in capital letters.

This WAS "Gina's street! The power of Visualization!

3. **Gina Moving into Apartment: "VISUALIZED"**

The next coincidence that occurred was after signing the lease, Gina met a former high school classmate on the same street of her apartment. It was a nice greeting to think Gina would have a friend to call upon if needed unfortunately he was leaving that weekend for the military. We then needed to get back on the road for Cape Cod and our vacation.

Later that week when we needed to move Gina to Boston, we filled the SUV with the new mattress, new apartment essentials and 8 weeks' worth of food. Our son was only with us for the weekend which meant we didn't have any physical help moving Gina in. In route to Boston, I told Gina it would be great if she ran into her classmate again so that we had someone to help us unload and move all the boxes and bed up the many flights of stairs. Gina reminded her me however, that her friend would have already left for the military.

No more than five minutes after I verbalized that desire, the friend texted Gina stating he was still in Boston because the military delayed his departure a week. He even offered to help her move in. He met us outside the entrance to Gina's apartment building and helped us move everything up the ten flights of stairs.

Here lies the third amazing visualization to manifest itself into reality, wow!
Talk about the "Power of Visualization!"

As a father, it still amazes me each and every time when I see one of my children's visualization become a real physical reality. It is truly unbelievable.

For further support of this concept of creative visualization and the power it has, I would like to share a story about a comedian who you all know well, Jim Carrey.

Here is the Jim Carrey $10 Million Creative Visualization story;

The following story has been written about in several media, including a video of The Oprah Winfrey program. "A financially broke Jim Carrey wrote a check to himself for $10 million in 1987. He dated the check for Thanksgiving 1995, and added a note "for services rendered."

On the day when Jim's father died, he tossed the check into the casket and considered it to only be a matter of time before he had the $10 million in his possession and a few short years later, he did have it. He visualized what he wanted and in 1994 he received $10 million for his role in Dumb and Dumber."

While these actions may not seem as significant as the years that he spent working on his acting career, it is likely that they played a large role in influencing his conviction that the money will be forthcoming. Jim Carrey is one of the most well paid actors in Hollywood.

Visualization has been an important tool for many successful individuals. Below are additional quotes from names you may recognize but would have never known that their success was derived from visualization.

How Other Rich & Famous Persons Use Creative Visualization

"I visualized where I wanted to be, what kind of player I wanted to become.
I knew exactly where I wanted to go, and I focused on getting there."
~ Michael Jordan

"The mind is really so incredible. Before I won my first Mr. Universe title, I walked
around the tournament like I owned it. I had won it so many times in my mind,
the title was already mine. "Then when I moved on to the movies I used the same
technique. I visualized daily being a successful actor and earning big money."
~ Arnold Schwarzenegger

"I have used visualization as a tool for a successful career for years. I see myself
doing what it is I want, and do not let go of this picture until it manifests."
~ Suzanne Somers

"In my mind, I've always been an A-list Hollywood superstar.
Y'all just didn't know yet."
~ Will Smith

"Dreaming is not enough. You have to go a step further and use your imagination
to visualize, with intent! Forget everything you've ever been taught, and believe it
will happen, just as you imagined it. That is the secret. That is the mystery of life."
~ Christine Anderson

"I believe people can move things with their minds."
~ Justin Timberlake

In addition to these celebrity stories, I would like to share with you my ten year visualization experience. Here is a powerful example that brings together both writing your ten-year goals and the use of creative visualization to make it happen. This is another real life example that helped motivate me to write this book and share this story with people around the world.

Dennis' Powerful Visualization of Third TEN Year Plan:

I had grown to understand the power and the magnitude of what could be delivered in one's life using creative visualization and I fully embraced making that happen. I started on the floor of the family room of my sister-in-law's house in Phoenix Arizona where I was feverishly detailing out each of the ten years of this third ten-year plan by subject, and in as much complete detail as I could. From that starting point, and over the next eighteen months, I refined the work and more importantly I visualized frequently what I had written down. I visualized not just achieving the visualization but feeling and living that visualization.

The theme for this third ten-year plan was called "Maximum Return on Investment," preparing for my mid-life 40th birthday. This third ten-year plan built off the first ten year plan in which I completed three different work experiences to become a "well-rounded corporate man." That first ten year plan gave me invaluable real-world work experience. The second ten-year plan was focused on "Personal Development," in which I extended my studies in my learning beyond the traditional academic schooling. These learnings helped to groom me for the corporate world.

With the completion of both the first and the second ten-year plans, I had concluded it was time for me to move on and leverage these experiences and learnings into a package that would give me maximum return. With my written third ten year plan and my creative visualization of achieving it, I submitted a four-page letter and resume to a consulting firm, asking to become a partner with their group.

In the letter I outlined the following four components;
    I.   My past ten-year plans
    II.   What I have to offer the consulting firm
    III. My next ten-year plan
    IV. What I envisioned for my future

The end of the story is that I received a phone call at 2 PM in the middle of my 40th year birthday party from the founder & partner of the consulting firm. He was calling in response to my letter and he indicated there was a mutual interest in working with me. He wanted to determine the next steps for the two of us. That phone call was truly a manifestation of a year and half of creative visualization. Today, this third ten year plan has been completed and exceeded my written objectives. ***This stuff works!***

I've discovered that numerous peak performers use the skill of mental rehearsal of visualization . . .
They mentally run through important events before they happen.
~ Charles A. Garfield, Clinical Professor & Author

TAKEAWAYS: Visualization

- There is no limit to what a person can achieve through visualization once the person gets past the denial state and embraces visualization.

- Visualizing a goal is the first step to achieving it.

- Start visualizing with a simple goal and then advance to a more complex goal.

- Creative visualization is the most powerful tool to your success.

Reviewing what you have completed in previous exercises is important for this next exercise with visualization. Your written ten year plan has already impacted on your subconscious mind and your actions. You now want to take your goals and manifest them into reality. How do you go about doing this? The exercise in this step is designed to walk you through the use of creative visualization.

Before you begin, you need to calm your mind and find a quiet place where you will be uninterrupted. This exercise will be effective only if you immerse yourself into this process.

Let's get started!

You will now be given the instructions of how to use creative visualization and two examples of visualization, a small goal and a more significant goal.

Exercise #5: Creative Visualization

Objective:

- To visualize a goal. Produce results through visualizing what you want or need, whether it be a simple desire or a grandiose dream.

Steps:

- Refer back to your dreams and goals worksheet. Select one of the goals as a starting point.
- You must clearly state your goal before you begin this process. It can be a simple one to start with, such as obtaining recognition for something you are looking to accomplish or measurable results for something you need. Or it can be of significant importance whereas you will need strong concentration and repetitive visualization to produce the desired results.
- It is now time for you to get comfortable in that quiet area you have chosen. Take a few strong breaths and then breathe away any negative thoughts. Calm yourself.
- Imagine yourself where you need to be in relationship to your goal to start this visualization of success. Take note of your feelings, emotions, smell, sounds, temperature, taste and all other specifics related to your present situation. As you see yourself in this vision, take note of what you are wearing and your total appearance.
- You are now ready to advance through your visualization journey. Using all of the same senses, begin your interaction with your environment and those in your vision. All of your senses need to be involved with this activity. Start advancing through your visual activities that are required before you can reach your desired goal. Present yourself exactly as you want to produce the results you desire.
- The important ingredient here is detail and your emotional immersion into the visualization. *For the purpose of this exercise,* once you have reached your goal, you will then need to record everything you just visualized. The first thing you record is the specific goal or objective of this visualization. You then need to use the same extreme detail as you visualized and put it into writing. Your environment, senses, moods, interactions, etc. Detail, detail, detail. This written exercise is not required for all your visualizations but rather is used as a teaching tool for this exercise. This does not need to be rewritten every day as you visualize, although it would provide greater energy towards manifesting your dream into a reality.
- Repetitive visualization is the key to its success. You need to believe and repeat this action over and over again until it manifests into your reality.

Example #1: Small Goal: VISUALIZATION EXAMPLE

Identify Goal:

Sell a scooter on Craig's List by the end of the day.

State what you are feeling and then experience it through all your senses. Your sense of touch, smell, taste, hearing and seeing while visualizing yourself obtaining and achieving your end goal.

Sit down in a quiet spot first thing in the morning and clearly express your desire to sell the "product" (for this example we will use a scooter). See yourself receiving phone calls, text messages, and emails from different individuals expressing interest in the scooter. Hear yourself responding to these individuals and encouraging them to come out and test drive the scooter.

Witness the people driving up your driveway and walking into your garage with you to see the scooter. See the excitement in their eyes and watch their body language that says to you they really want this scooter! Call them by name and hear them use your name while talking with you. Hear and see yourself negotiating on the price but standing firm that this is the best price you can give them.

You know from the excitement in their eyes and their body language that they are still going to purchase the product at your price. Watch as they nod their heads, confirming their desire to buy your product. You now see them reach into their pocket and pull out ten and twenty dollar bills and watch them count their money. As they hand the money to you, feel the crispness of the bills and rub your fingers over the money as you take it from them.

Feel how heavy the scooter is as you help load it into the buyer's car. Now watch the car and scooter drive away from your home. You personally feel the excitement of joy in your body and mind that you have actually sold the product and received the cash. Rejoice over successfully selling your scooter and know that it was this visualization that helped make it happen.

Creative Visualization

Identify Your Goal:

_____

State what you are feeling and then experience it through all your senses. Your sense of touch, smell, taste, hearing and seeing while visualizing yourself obtaining and achieving your end goal.

Example #2: Complex Goal: <u>VISUALIZATION EXAMPLE</u>

Identify Goal:

Visualize yourself being selected and promoted to the next position on your career ladder. With more complex visualization, you need to repetitively visualize and see it physically unfolding over time until the final objective is reached.

State what you are feeling and then experience it through all your senses. Your sense of touch, smell, taste, hearing and seeing while visualizing yourself obtaining and achieving your end goal.

Visualize yourself attending meetings in which you are called upon to ask for your input and suggestions on how to deal with challenges within your organization. Feel the anxiety that comes over your body as you are about to speak. Hear yourself responding to these questions and then getting positive feedback by those in attendance of the meeting, as well as by the supervisor running the meeting. Feel your face tingle and your body shake from the excitement of being respected. You hear responses such as "that really makes sense," "that will really work," "we really need to try this approach," etc. After leaving the meeting you receive a memo that your approach and ideas are going to be implemented. Now visualize the positive results happening in the organization based on your input and suggestions. This is generating positive enthusiasm within the company.

Visualize being invited by your boss to attend his boss's meetings. See yourself over time being asked for your input and suggestions from those in attendance. Repeat feeling some nervousness first and then more self-confidence. See your input and suggestions being well received by those in the meetings. Again more importantly, you start to see positive results happening in the organization based on your recommendations.

As you proceed through this visualization you now can see yourself being called into your boss's office and asked to sit down. Your boss shares that you have been selected for the promotion you have desired on your career ladder. You feel excitement overwhelm your mind and body as you digest what is happening. Then your boss walks around and extends his hand to give you a congratulations shake recognizing your promotion. You can feel the firmness and the body warmth of his hand as you shake. You can see the sparkle of excitement in his eyes and you know he's genuinely excited for you.

As you drive home and walk into your home, see yourself greeted by your spouse or someone special. Express to them you have an announcement to share. You then announce with great excitement your new position on your career ladder. More importantly, you see the sparkle in their eyes and sincere smile on their face. You can feel their hands and arms hug you in congratulations of your significant accomplishment. You have successfully completed your visualization in your mind. And then you repeat this daily until you receive that promotion.

Creative Visualization / COMPLEX IMAGE

Identify Your <u>Complex</u> Goal:

_____

_____

State what you are feeling and then experience it through all your senses. Your sense of touch, smell, taste, hearing and seeing while visualizing yourself obtaining and achieving your end goal.

STEP 6

Cloud of Unknowing
"Mentors / Role Models"

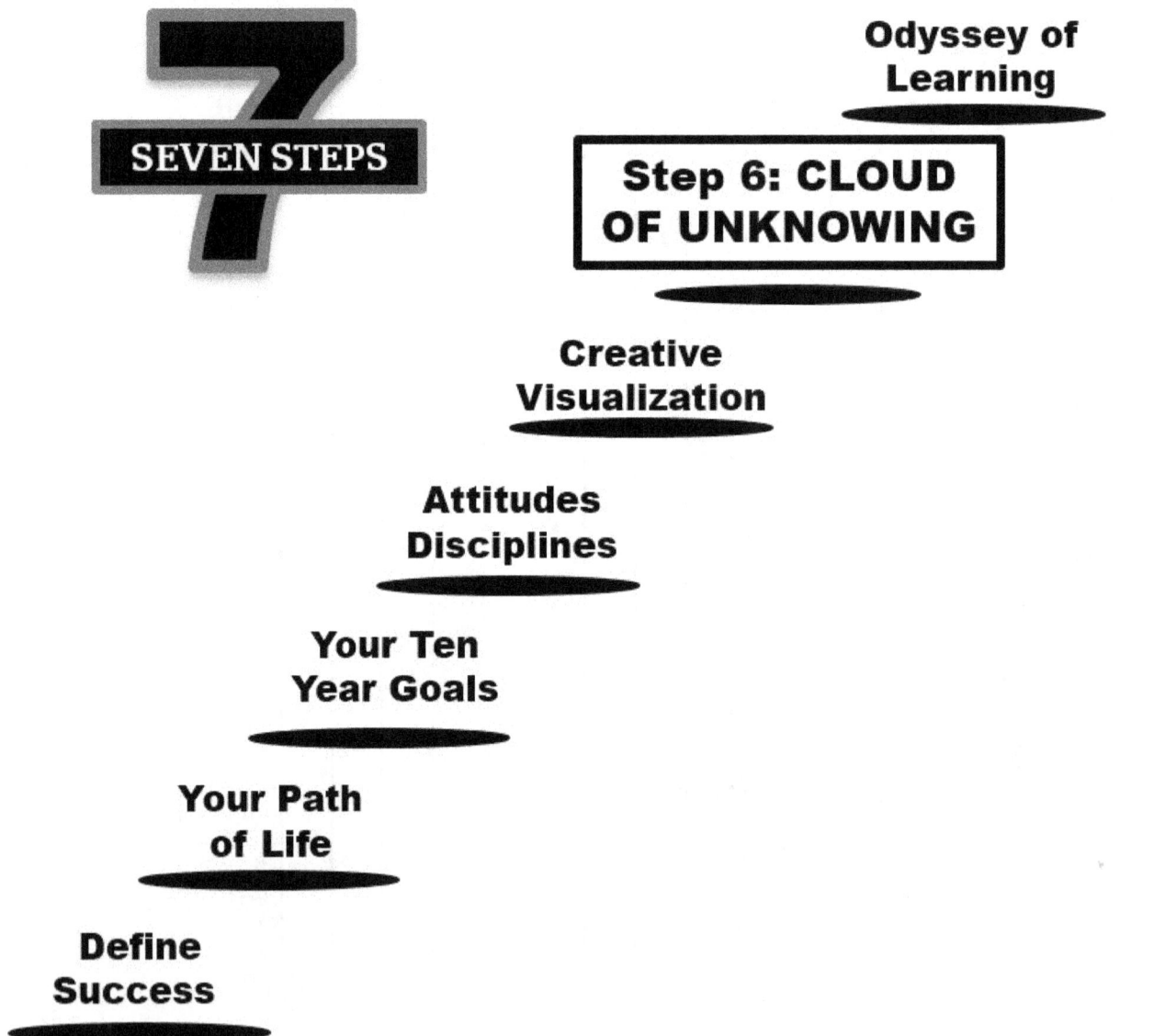

SEVEN STEPS 7

Odyssey of Learning

Step 6: CLOUD OF UNKNOWING

Creative Visualization

Attitudes Disciplines

Your Ten Year Goals

Your Path of Life

Define Success

Everybody is ignorant, only on different subjects.
~ Will Rogers, Columnist, Commentator & Actor

Ignorance is bliss, or so they say. If this were true, the world would be in a heap of trouble. There would be no passion for learning, no thirst for knowledge, and little chance for personal growth.

You may have realized very early on when your education began that there is a great deal to learn in life. The learning process is not over when you graduate from high school or college. It is an ongoing process. There is a lot to be gained by having a personal development plan at every stage in your life. Successful people know this as they continue to learn from family, friends, mentors, competitors and experts in their field. The quest for personal growth should never stop!

Therefore, this step will introduce key sources that will influence your quest for personal growth, they are; mentors, roles models and networking. Before we can discuss these sources, we first need to establish the concept of the unknown.

The "Cloud of Unknowing"

"We don't know what we do not know." For purposes of this book, the "Cloud of Unknowing" refers to areas of knowledge you are unaware of, and it also refers to the skills you need to acquire that you may not know you need. Some of the greatest risks we face in life are these "Clouds of Unknowing." You can quantify what your strengths and weaknesses are in various topics if you are aware of the topics. It's what you don't know that can sometimes sabotage you.

Something like this occurred when my wife Patricia and I bought our first house. It's an interesting story to illustrate because it taught us a valuable lesson.

Dennis' Cloud of Unknowing

Patricia and I were young and newly married when we decided to build our first home. After months of haggling with the building contractor, we got him down to a great price and signed the contract. We knew we had a great price, but "we didn't know what we did not know." We didn't know what we should have known about building specifications. Yes the obvious was discussed such as the width of wood frame, the standardized cabinets, floors, windows, etc. However we were foreign to most of the structural specifications and hence, we got the lowest specifications on the house. Because we had gotten a great price, we were happy—naive to what had happened, but happy; that is, until about 7 years later when everything in the house started to fall apart and we had to repair or replace structural issues.

When it came time to buy our second, larger home, we knew what to ask for in building specifications. We negotiated the building specifications in addition to having great concerns about the price. Why? Because we now knew about building specifications, something we did not know about the first time we built a home. The "cloud of unknowing" had lifted.

In reality, we needed to consult with someone who was experienced and knowledgeable about construction considering it is one of the largest purchases one makes in their lives. We all need people in our lives who can assist us with different clouds of unknowing.

This example of the "cloud of unknowing" is an important lead into our next subject, which is mentors. Mentorship is a valuable asset. Mentors often identify a particular "cloud of unknowing" before you get too far off track or are about to make a big blunder. Just having the "cloud of unknowing" exposed to you can give you a competitive advantage in many situations, let alone unveil an area of expertise you are missing.

Education is learning what you didn't even know you didn't know.
~ Daniel Boorstin, American Historian & Author

Three Components / Unveil the Cloud of Unknowing

There are three components we will look at in this step that offer you the resources to help you unveil the cloud of unknowing. They are ***mentors, role models, and networking.***

A good approach to moving forward on your path of life is to secure **mentors** to work with and then choose appropriate **role models** to emulate. To leverage this further, I recommend **building a network** of non-mentor resources in the areas you are lacking expertise. Non-mentor resources are individuals who are neither mentors nor role models; they are key resources. These individuals become an important part of your network, in fact having a key resource person would have helped in our decision-making with building our home. These components will be valuable assets during your success journey.

Mentors

Before sharing examples of mentor-mentee relationships, let's examine the definition and qualities to look for in a mentor. The dictionary definition of a "mentor" is; *a wise and trusted counselor or teacher; an influential senior sponsor or supporter.* My definition of a mentor is one who nurtures and helps in the development of another person by the giving of his or her time, knowledge, expertise and resources to the mentee.

Considering a mentor will be very influential in your life, it is important to identify qualities to look for in a mentor. Bearing in mind that surrounding yourself with positive people is a core to our teachings, the first quality is being a positive thinker. Remember, positive people attract positive energy.

It would have to be a person who is interested in providing you with new learnings, and the willingness to share with you their knowledge and expertise. You may admire many people however not all individuals are intended to be mentors. A mentor-mentee relationship may develop informally or through a formal mentoring program set up by a company. In an organization, mentors focus on career growth through better understanding of the business and/or company's structure. They provide a teaching environment usually designed towards the mission of the organization. Mentors may even be instrumental in mentees discovering and following new ambitions. Mentors can be found anywhere in a company where expertise exists, within executives, managers, and even peers.

Finding mentors within your family or other personal situations is certainly an option. The older generations in families tend to nurture their cultural backgrounds of the extended family members, often teaching from their own experiences and family-based learnings. After all, that is how traditions are passed from generation to generation. Close friendships foster mentoring relationships, often when there is an age difference. The point is regardless of your life situation, you can find a mentor for all your learning needs.

A good mentor accepts the responsibility of grooming their mentee. What do I mean by this? A good mentor will be a guiding force who offers you insights on your strengths and weaknesses and then will offer constructive feedback on how to use your strengths and improve upon your weaknesses. He or she will follow your progress and provide their wisdom and expertise to influence your personal and/or professional growth.

Someone who is really interested in mentoring will be an integral part of your growth plan. The mentor will insist on goals and disciplines that will encourage your success in life. This mentor will expect what he or she expects from themselves, often challenging you to rise to their degree of expertise. He/she is a motivator and achiever, inspiring you to raise the bar as you progress in your learning curve.

You want to be associated with someone who emulates integrity, trustworthiness, intelligence, open-mindedness and kind-heartedness. Someone who is respected by peers and superiors. An individual who offers constructive criticism and supportive direction.

         www.achievingsuccesscenter.com

Every one of you reading this can probably name at least one person you have met who made a difference in your life and held one or more of these qualities. It could be a sixth grade teacher who saw some potential in you that you didn't even know existed. Perhaps you were fortunate in your first job to have an upper level executive take an interest in your growth and development. Whatever the case may be, a mentor can be your career's most important ally or the catalyst to personal growth in areas of interest.

Writing this book and giving seminars is part of our mentoring program; that is, providing learning tools that will sharpen your skills and motivate you to achieving your definition of success. Why do we think mentoring is so important? Because I have been both mentee and mentor, and I know first-hand that my successes have been influenced by the number of great mentors in my life. I appreciate all their wisdom, patience, time and energy they invested in teaching me new concepts and techniques that increased my growth both in my personal and career life.

Mentorship is a giving process. The mentor, as well as the mentee, benefits from the mentoring role. For example, the mentor may gain a better understanding of other kinds of work styles or acquire new technical skills while being a mentor to another. Since mentors are usually advanced in their professions, the very act of mentoring can be regenerating to the mentor's career interests and aspirations. Mentoring also develops the mentor's network of contacts. Most mentors simply derive satisfaction from passing their knowledge on to others.

The time you spend with a mentor is a key ingredient to keeping you focused on your goals and disciplines in attaining them. Depending on your mentor's own development cycle you may continue to grow with your mentor or it's not uncommon to outgrow your mentor after two or three years. It is at that time you should seek out your next mentor. You can also have a lifetime mentor, someone who you continue to learn from and hold in high regard. I am lucky enough to have two such mentors in my life today.

Some guidelines for a successful mentoring relationship are:
- Acknowledge the sacrifice a mentor is making on your behalf.
- Utilize your mentor's time effectively and take advantage of their wisdom and experiences.
- Ask questions, learn from their expertise and observe their manner.
- Mentoring relationships may end sooner than expected, be prepared.
- Express appreciation to your mentor both during and after the mentoring years.

Those who wish to improve their relationship with others, or want to cultivate healthier, more harmonious and compassionate relationships in general, will benefit from the mentoring process.

Examples of Famous People and Their Mentors
Most successful people credit their mentors for their successes.

Oprah Winfrey, an American media proprietor, talk show host, actress, producer, and philanthropist, shares these thoughts about her mentor, Maya Angelou. *"She was there for me always, guiding me through some of the most important years of my life," "The world knows her as a poet but at the heart of her, she was a teacher. 'When you learn, teach. When you get, give' is one of my best lessons from her."* Written by Oprah after the death of her mentor.

Michael Jordan, an American former professional basketball player, businessman, and principal owner and chairman of the Charlotte Hornets, shared these words about his mentor, Coach Dean Smith; *"Other than my parents, no one had a bigger influence on my life than Coach Smith. He was more than a coach – he was my mentor, my teacher, my second father. Coach was always there for me whenever I needed him and I loved him for it. In teaching me the game of basketball, he taught me about life."*

Warren Buffet, an American business magnate, investor and philanthropist, took on the role of mentor for Katherine Graham, an American publisher. She led her family's newspaper, The Washington Post, for more than two decades. Katherine Graham met Warren Buffet in the early 1970's during her tenure as CEO of The Washington Post Company. In 1971 Buffet bought a large piece of the company. In her autobiography, *Personal History,* Katherine Graham pays tribute to Warren Buffet when she writes, "By the spring of 1974, Warren was sending me a constant flow of helpful memos and advice, and occasionally alerting me to problems of which I was unaware. In the beginning I didn't realize how fortunate I was to have this mentor, but I grew very dependent on his advice, and liked it. In effect, he was beginning to teach me the fundamentals of thinking about business, for which I had so longed."

After Buffet was made a board member of the company in September of 1974, Katherine got even further educated by her mentor. "With most things regarding the business side of the company, I still felt uncomfortable, fragile, and vulnerable. Here, Warren really went to work on me. My business education began in earnest—he literally took me to business school. Which was just what I needed. How lucky I was to be educated—to the extent possible—by Warren Buffet, and how many people would have given anything for the same experience. It was hard work for both of us—Warren admitted I needed what he called 'a little remedial work'—but absolutely vital for me." Although a close personal relationship is not a prerequisite for good mentoring, Graham and Buffet clearly had a great friendship as well as a notable and long-standing mentor-protégé relationship.

It isn't difficult to find famous people who have been inspired by their mentors, but what about the rest of us, who don't have the notoriety of the celebrities but have been motivated to do great things by our mentors. For instance, how many of you can recall family members, friends, or persons in your workplace who have provided you with some degree of mentorship. Often these mentors in your life are not recognized for their roles until you are much older and wiser about life.

Let me share with you some of my mentors, although not famous to you, are legendary to me.

Mentor – Personal Development

The following is an example of my first mentor in life, my Uncle Harry. My Uncle Harry lived next door to my grandmother's house, and he helped fill some of the male figurehead voids after my father and grandfather both died. He particularly helped me gain confidence in myself by showing me how to build things with my hands.

One summer he suggested we build a 16' x 24' above ground, redwood swimming pool on the vacant lot my mother owned next door to us. It was a huge undertaking in the eyes of a teenage boy, but Uncle Harry patiently demonstrated how to pre-plan a project of this size. We had to survey the empty lot, order truckloads of sand and steel support beams, and build a prototype to mass produce thirty-two side support wings which would hold up the side walls of the pool. We accomplished all this in fourteen days. The teachings I learned went beyond building something with my hands, it was the skills of project management, it was the rewards of hard work, and it was about bonding, cooperation and respect that goes along with working side by side with a mentor. Uncle Harry, as my mentor, identified a number of *clouds of unknowing* related to this project and was instrumental in filling these voids of knowledge.

Nineteen years later, when my uncle was on his deathbed, I reminded him of that great pool project we had completed together. Tears flowed down both our faces as I told him how proud I was of that project. I will never forget my first mentor.

Mentor – Career Development

When I moved up the career ladder into middle management with the regional supermarket chain, I knew I needed a business mentor. Mike, an executive with the company, showed interest in me and I had a reciprocal desire for him as my mentor. I was fortunate that Mike established this mentoring role and that he possessed all the qualities listed above that one would search for in a mentor. He identified my weaknesses in the areas of the essential skills needed for my growth, the knowledge necessary to assume higher management positions, and the overall experience crucial for senior management. Mike exposed me to all facets of the business that were required of upper management. Mike understood my desired goals of continuing up the career ladder and he mentored me, offering me learning experiences and business teachings that are invaluable to me even today.

I would like to share with you one particular business process that was a highlight in my career. Mike provided me with the freedom and guidance needed to author and execute my first written Master Business Plan. It was a business plan to completely reorganize the Grocery department and to redefine and streamline its work flow process. I worked hard for weeks on this plan and submitted it to Mike for his approval upon its completion. What I received back was not at all what I expected, it was completely covered in red-ink. The red-inked areas were Mike's proposed revisions. This process of resubmitting over and over again and then receiving back continuous versions with more red ink remarks went on for at least three months. It was grueling, to say the least. However, by the end of it, I had one complete Master Business Plan—and it was successfully implemented! Talk about achieving a career milestone, this propelled me to become the director of the grocery department, responsible for one billion dollars in sales. I have my mentor, "red-ink Mike" to thank for this milestone.

That period of mentorship was an excellent career growth opportunity because I proved to myself that my persistency and focus towards any endeavor I choose could be successful. I owe my retail business expertise to Mike, who became more to me than just a great mentor, he was my teacher, my counselor, and my life-long friend. Mike, as my mentor, opened doors to many *clouds of unknowing* throughout my work relationship with him and continues to do so even today as we remain lifelong friends.

Mentor – Business Consulting Development

If you recall in Step 5, I visualized my next third ten year plan to become a business consultant and I sent my four page resume letter to a specific individual in a consulting group. In doing so, I gained a wonderful mentor and friend Brian, founder and partner of the business consulting group. Brian was the consultant who contacted me during my 40th birthday party. You see, our mentor-mentee relationship began that day. Brain was the business consultant guru who took me under his wing to mold and groom me for the retail business portion of his international consulting firm. Talk about feeling inadequate. Here I am, a young businessman who has always had the security of a company's "mother hen", now leading the charge of a retail division as an independent consultant. It would be an understatement to suggest I needed professional growth and grooming for this new career, as my cloud of unknowing was enormous. Brian took an interest in both my personal and professional life, always encouraging a balance between them both.

What did I learn from this experience? Having the right mentor can be your ticket to success! Brian was that mentor to me. He was also the epitome of a successful role model. His professionalism and integrity was second to none and his charismatic manner and wisdom was the key to securing client engagements. Brian taught me every aspect of the consulting business and opened my eyes to all the unknowns in this field of work. His patience and guidance was unwavering, inspiring my enthusiasm for growth and motivating improvement of my weaknesses. He taught me how to work with clients and develop customized products and services to meet their needs. I learned invaluable lessons and tools on how to deliver results!

We have traveled the world visiting 6 continents and a dozen countries while working for numerous retail and manufacturing clients. I owe my business consulting success to this great mentor who exposed the *clouds of unknowing* and provided me with the expertise and knowledge needed. Beyond mentorship, we continue to be lifetime friends.

Mentors have influenced my success at different points in my life. Each one of them has influenced my life and motivated me to achieve many of my goals. Mentors can be such an important part of one's overall success that finding, enlisting and maximizing mentors in your life should be considered a priority so that you learn from them as early into your life as possible.

Role Models

While a mentor is an individual you learn from and you are actively involved with, a role model is someone you learn from and emulate, but you are not actively involved with them. In fact, most often the role model has no knowledge of you nor of your learning from them. The definition of a role model is; *a person looked to by others as an example to be imitated.*

We would like it if our parents were outstanding role models for us, but unfortunately that isn't always true. My mother was a fiercely independent woman who could stand on her own. She was never afraid to take on life's challenges, so for me, she exemplified what courage, determination and independence stood for. I was very fortunate to have such a role model in my life.

Most of us need to look outside the family for role models. The challenge is the world offers us both positive and negative role models. Many of our young people are influenced and motivated by too many negative role models. That's why it is important to recognize some of the qualities of a good role model.

- **Motivate/Inspire:** A role model should motivate you to succeed and inspire you to be the best at whatever you are emulating from that individual.

- **Values:** Upholding ethical and moral values is key to a good society. This should be paramount in the virtues of a good role model.

- **Creativity/Uniqueness:** Role models have a great effect on the ingenuity and creativeness of others.

- **Ambition:** A role model who is ambitious and successful tends to influence career objectives of people looking for the same. They make the impossible, possible.

- **Leadership:** Our world sensationalizes disasters of all types, and the manner in which a role model handles themselves during a crisis has a huge impact on others behavior and emotions.

- **Good Character:** Individuals display solid principles, integrity, and strong work ethics.

Please keep in mind that no individual is perfect and therefore, even the best role models will have flaws.

Below are examples of some role models who are admired in their field of expertise.

A role model is one whose traits you admire and who you can learn from by example.

1. Carli Lloyd – Excellent role model for a young girl playing soccer.
2. Mother Teresa – Charitable role model for all caregivers.
3. Will Smith – Role model for young boys who needs encouragement as musician or actor.
4. Oprah Winfrey – Inspiring role model for all young women to reach their full potential.
5. Carrie Underwood – Role model for all struggling musicians that success can come to those starting from grassroots.
6. Susan Boyle – Heartwarming role model for persons who don't feel the glamour in their lives yet earn respect based on talent.
7. Pope Francis – Spiritual role model for all believers to have hope.
8. Bill Gates – Entrepreneur and philanthropist role model who represents ambition and success, along with charitable acts and generosity.
9. J.K. Rowling – Author, of Harry Potter book series, role model to future aspiring authors.
10. Steven Spielberg – Movie Producer role model for ambitious hopeful movie makers.

Role Model – Carli Lloyd

As a role model, Carli Lloyd amplifies what we have taught in this book about dreams turning into reality through visualization. Carli shot the winning goals for the Women's Soccer World Cup games in 2015. When interviewed, she publicly attributes her recent Women's World cup success on her dreams and specific visualization of how she would perform during the World games. As reported by USA Today Sports in the July 6, 2015 issue, Carli, while running on her own in May 2015, visualized scoring four or five goals during the June 2015 Women's World Cup games. Her on-field determination to change her dreams and visualization into physical reality was seen by the entire world. Carli used many of the methods taught in this book to achieve the success of scoring a hat trick of three goals in 16 minutes for the championship at the World Cup games. She explains how she set her goals for the game, used creative visualization as a tool to prepare for the game, and then shared how her mindset manifested into physical reality. Carli's dream became her reality.

Role Model – Carrie Underwood

The music industry is competitive and driven by fame, and many musicians fail under this pressure. That's why when Carrie Underwood, a hometown girl born on March 10 1983 in Muskogee Oklahoma on a farm rises to stardom, the world is fascinated by this journey. Despite her fame, Carrie remains rooted in her family and faith and when asked about being a role model for other aspiring young musicians by OK magazine, she is quoted saying, "My motto is, I would never want to do anything that would embarrass my own children in the future." She continues to say, "I never want to do anything that would make my parents, my role models, disappointed in me," Carrie could easily fall into the pattern of late party nights and tabloid coverage that one finds on the magazine racks, but instead, she remains music driven yet humble, wanting to portray a strong heart and positive image to all those who look up to her as a role model.

Role Model – Bill Gates

Being one of the richest men in the world does not qualify for being a good role model. It's what a person does with their success that brings them notoriety as a role model. In 1975, Bill Gates and Paul Allen founded Microsoft, with very little resources and converting a garage into their office space. From there the founder of Microsoft rose to fame and fortune. So yes, as an entrepreneur he could be considered a great role model, but there is a side to Bill Gates that is more deserving as a role model then the measure of his wealth. Bill Gates is a visionary and philanthropist. He is a business leader who believes in giving more than what he earns. Bill and Melinda Gates Foundation tackles global health issues and has contributed over $36 billion to fight hunger and disease. Both Bill and his wife have received awards dedicated to charitable work/affiliations with special causes, and will continue to be award recipients for their philanthropy. If your son or daughter wants to emulate the success and charitable nature of Bill, considered it ambitious and admirable!

Role models come in all sizes and walks of life. Don't think that you can only emulate a person who is famous or wealthy, absolutely not. If you can find individuals who possess the qualities discussed in this step, then you have found a good role model. You may find a good role model in your next door neighbor or in a friend of a friend. You can have several role models at once. The important thing is to choose role models who have the qualities listed and are successful in your field of interest. Then it's up to you to learn from the traits that made them successful.

TESTIMONIAL

Lic. Olga Esthela Quiroz Ruiz,
Director of Merchandising, Casa Ley

"We have collaborated with Dennis at Casa Ley for the last 13 years, mostly on the Business Field with outstanding results. Finally 4 years ago the collaboration expanded to Dennis' "Achieving Life and Career Success" Seminar, exceeding all the expectations we had. Directors, Managers and Middle Management have experienced it with great results in both their work, but mainly on their personal lives, being this a driver for success at Casa Ley.

Personally it has been a pleasure to work with a person like Dennis. He is not an "academic" he is a full practitioner of all the concepts he shares in his seminars.

TAKEAWAYS: Mentors, Role Models and Networking

- Understanding the concept of "The Cloud of Unknowing" presents a mindset open to mentorship.

- Having mentors in your life will support you on your journey by giving you new learnings, confidence, direction, discipline, motivation on your chosen path, as well as fill in the voids of knowledge.

- Maintaining role models will encourage enthusiasm and a passion for you to emulate success.

- Building a network of individuals in many fields of interest will help you gain knowledge and bring forth opportunities.

- Expressing gratitude is a powerful tool and should be extended to mentors or individuals you assisted in your accomplishments.

How does one go about finding mentors and role models? This next exercise will help you identify these key individuals in your life. There are two worksheets, one for mentors and the second for role models. The steps in completing these worksheets are the same however it is suggested that you complete the mentor worksheet first and then advance to the role model chart.

Exercise #6: Selecting Mentors and Role Models

Objective:
- Identify the key mentors and role models that have assisted you in the past, and target future mentors and role models you will need.

Steps:
- In the left column list the names of those individuals considered to be mentors or instrumental in your personal and/or career growth. Reflect back to early childhood, then present day, and finally future mentor needs.

- Circle back to your ten year plan, list your desired position in life across the next ten years. Use this as an indicator of the type of mentor that will be necessary for that period of your life.

- Once identified, determine dates or time frame of mentor relationships, including future mentors. Also record your age or anticipated age range.

- The mentor's involvement should reflect the skill sets you have developed during your relationship as mentor-mentee.

- After completing the mentor chart, use the same approach to complete the role model chart and match this chart to your ten year plan.

EXAMPLE: Past – Current – Future MENTORS

MENTOR	TIME PERIOD	YOUR AGE	POSITION in LIFE	MENTOR'S INVOLVEMENT
Uncle Harry	1962 - 1970	8 - 16	Teenage growing years	Demonstrated how to physically build & create with my hands.
Ted	1972 - 1975	18 - 21	Store Manager	Leadership role & management skills.
Gary	1980 - 1983	26 - 29	Retail Buyer	Expertise of procurement
John	1983 - 1986	29 - 32	Asst. Director of Grocery	Total departmental responsibilities & knowledge
Nick	1988 - 1994	34 - 40	Director of Grocery	Developing as a well groomed director using a defined leadership process.
Mike	1986 - ongoing	32 - ongoing	Director of Grocery	Strategic planning with defined tactical execution equals results.
Brian	1994 - ongoing	40- ongoing	Retail Consultant	Project management to define & deliver results in retail client engagements.
Manuel	2009 - ongoing	55 - ongoing	Retail Executive	Understanding Mayan time & universal wisdom
Gerry	2015 - 2017	60+	Author / Consultant	Need author with book writing expertise
TBD	Future	60+	Author / Consultant	Online social media / marketing
TBD	Future	60+	Author / Consultant	Online product selling

Past – Current – Future MENTORS

MENTOR	TIME PERIOD	YOUR AGE	POSITION in LIFE	MENTOR'S INVOLVEMENT

EXAMPLE: Past - Current - Future ROLE MODELS

ROLE MODEL	TIME PERIOD	YOUR AGE	YOUR POSITION IN LIFE	ROLE MODEL'S INVOLVEMENT
Brian	1978 - 1994	25 - 40	Career in Retail Management	Being an uncompromising ethics leader & motivator
Bob	1980 - 1994	28 - 40	Dir of Department - Major Corporation	Reflect faith principles in both your personal and professional life.
Sven	1996 - 1997	42 - 43	Retail Consultant	How to be more disciplined in my life to accomplish multiple goals.
Patricia	1975 - ongoing	20 - ongoing	Spouse	Defines sacrifice & a principle-guided life.
Mike	1980 - ongoing	28 - current	Retail Management	Strategic planning with defined tactical execution equals results.
Brian	1994 - ongoing	40 - ongoing	Retail Consultant	Project management to define & deliver results in retail client engagements.
Dave	2016	60+	Author / Consultant	Author & speaker with success model
Gandhi	2016 - 2017	60+	Author / Consultant	Desire to be a minimalist
TBD	Future	60+	Author / Consultant	King/Queen of social media for business
TBD	Future	60+	Author / Consultant	Award winning online product selling

www.achievingsuccesscenter.com

Past - Current - Future ROLE MODELS

ROLE MODEL	TIME PERIOD	YOUR AGE	YOUR POSITION IN LIFE	ROLE MODEL'S INVOLVEMENT

Networking

Let's face it, no one person is expected to know everything about all topics. We all have learning curves in many aspects of our lives. It's part of being human. We cannot be expected to be an expert in all these fields; tax law, refinancing, home repair, auto mechanics, relationships, conflict management, writing a book, etc.?

The term **networking** means *a supportive system of sharing information and services among individuals and groups having a common interest*. Each person in your network should offer you expertise, experience, exposure and resources related to their field of interest.

You maintain contact with this network of people whom you can tap into when you need their expertise and/or resources. In exchange, you remain available to them when they come to you for information and skills within your areas of expertise.

Networking guidelines:

- Be aware of the particular resources and skills you have, and share them openly and eagerly at every opportunity.

- Show appreciation when someone in your network lends you their expertise. A simple "thank you" note, letter, text, email or phone call acknowledging their assistance are good forms of gratitude.

- Identify the resources missing in your network and search for individuals who can complete your network. Be prepared to seize the opportunity to connect with these individuals when chance happens.

- Build your network by subject, by persons, or both.

- Become a greater giver than a taker. By doing so, you will invariably find that people are always ready and willing to assist you.

More often than not, you will find your network contacts within the framework of your business and social organization, or referrals. At times, you may need to go beyond that through outside organizations. Some additional sources of networking would include, professional and non-professional groups, regional and local chamber of commerce, regional and local trade associations, service and social organizations, public bureaus, etc. The important principle is to develop relationships with good resource experts in the area of your interest.

The delicate balance of mentoring someone is not creating them in your own image,
but giving them the opportunity to create themselves.
~ Steven Spielberg

TAKEAWAYS: Mentors, Role Models and Networking

- Understanding the concept of "The Cloud of Unknowing" presents a mindset open to mentorship.

- Having mentors in your life will support you on your journey by giving you new learnings, confidence, direction, discipline, motivation on your chosen path, as well as fill in the voids of knowledge.

- Maintaining role models will encourage enthusiasm and a passion for you to emulate success.

- Building a network of individuals in many fields of interest will help you gain knowledge and bring forth opportunities.

- Expressing gratitude is a powerful tool and should be extended to mentors or individuals you assisted in your accomplishments.

STEP 7

Odyssey of Learning
"Personal Development"

SEVEN STEPS 7

Step 7: ODYSSEY OF LEARNING

Cloud of
Unknowing

Creative
Visualization

Attitudes
Disciplines

Your Ten
Year Goals

Your Path
of Life

Define
Success

Live as if you were to die tomorrow. Learn as if you were to live forever.
~ Mahatma Gandhi, Leader of Indian independence movement

This step will focus on personal development and the concept we refer to as your own personal "Odyssey of Learning." Seek out individuals who are smarter than you and with greater insight into areas of learning that are of interest to you. Pursue areas that will help your personal growth as well as your career. Your growth will be dependent on your motivation and initiative to surround yourself with individuals who will introduce you to new learnings that you didn't even know existed. Thus, you begin the journey of your personal "Odyssey of Learning" and identify your new "Clouds of Unknowing."

Invest in Your Personal Development

Personal Development includes activities that improve awareness and identity, develop talents and potential, and position individuals to excel in their desired ambitions and goals in life. As we previously mentioned in Step 3, our ten year goal planning gives you time to fill the many voids of experience and learnings to achieve your ambitious goals. Your personal growth and development will focus on these voids as you create a detailed, individualized timeline of educational activities to provide the needed new learnings, skills, and expertise to move forward in your ten year plan. At this point you will have identified your weaknesses and threats in your SWOT in Step 2, along with your personal voids identified in your ten year plans. These findings will determine what type of learnings are needed and these educational activities should be scheduled over a one to three year period of time.

Personal Development - Timeline
Levels of Development

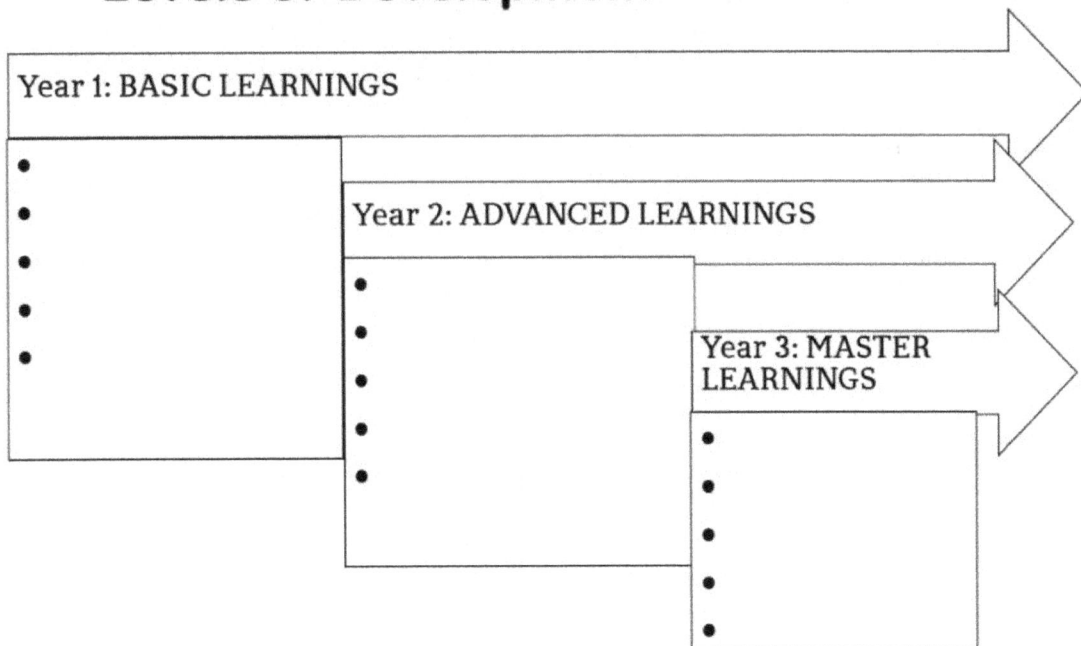

Year 1: BASIC LEARNINGS
-
-
-
-
-

Year 2: ADVANCED LEARNINGS
-
-
-
-
-

Year 3: MASTER LEARNINGS
-
-
-
-

At various times in my life, I have felt the need to broaden my horizons in terms of my personal and professional development. The main reason for this was to keep abreast of trends in my field of interest, address shortcomings in skill deficiencies, and sharpen my skills. In an effort to offer more clarity, I will share with you some of my personal development required to fill my experience and learning voids in my ten year goal setting.

As early as 1981, I participated in Dale Carnegie's "Effective Speaking and Human Relations" course. This course significantly changed my life for the better. As a youth, I was not very outgoing, but I realized when I entered the business world that I would have to expand my skills to deal with people in this fast-paced environment. I was totally amazed that I could learn so much from one course after college and that it could have such an impact on me. Carnegie's approach left such an indelible mark on me that in1987 I took the Dale Carnegie "Management Skills" training course and then in 1989 returned to Dale Carnegie to attend their "Leader in the Class" course. These first steps truly ignited my desire to continuously expand my personal development in as many different fields of interest that would assist me to achieve my ten year plan.

In 1988, I spent two days at a "Creativity and Innovation Studies" seminar. I learned that the left side of the brain takes a more detailed, structured, and accounting approach to things, and the right side is more creative, artistic, and open to ideas. This course helped me to open the right side of my brain, to be open-minded and creative. It exposed me to the concept of using both sides of my brain in situations, which often gives me a competitive edge over others who tend to use one side or the other.

Every year I try to enhance my talent and skills as an individual, speaker, and business owner through continuous scheduling of educational activities to fill my experience and learning voids and clouds of unknowing.

We live in the "information age." I imagine that virtually every field of interest that exists on this planet has been written about. If not, you can bet there is someone out there thinking of writing about it. There are books, audio tapes and seminars from which you can learn in a relatively short time what it took years for the author or speaker to learn.

What are you doing about your personal growth? Reading this book indicates that you are interested in acquiring the wisdom and knowledge you need to reach new pinnacles of success. I would venture to say that anything which improves your ability to think is worth pursuing. And this doesn't mean you have to go out and earn another college degree. Adult education courses at your local schools and colleges are great places for continued learning. They generally offer classes in everything from computer skills to the culinary arts. There are many good and informative online sites available in virtually every field of interest.

In addition to the traditional learnings, I encourage you to include alternative and non-traditional educational approaches in your journey. Some approaches to consider are one-on-one mentorship with unconventional thinkers, online video classes, offsite workshops, etc. Why are alternative learnings important? It is the extraordinary people who "think differently" and have the ability to develop unique solutions to complex problems or issues. Surround yourself with these individuals and they will introduce you to concepts that could provide you with universal wisdom.

TAKEAWAYS: Personal Development

- Create and implement a personal development plan that will assist in your life success plan.

- Continuous learning and self-improvement is necessary for success.

- There are numerous resources available to you for continued enlightenment in your fields of interest. Some include books, tapes, seminars, adult education courses, and the Internet.

- Include alternative and non-traditional educational approaches in your journey

Exercise #7: Personal Development

Objective:

- Identify the skills you need to learn and areas of knowledge you should explore in order to better implement your one-year and ten-year plans.

Steps:

- Reflect on your one year and ten year goals to identify what areas of knowledge or skill you need to improve that will assist in achieving those goals.

- Target three books to read and/or seminars to attend that will provide you with needed information and/or skills to advance in these fields of interest.

- Research what or who is available to provide you with the knowledge or skills needed. Determine how you can include this in your personal development plan.

- Schedule the time you need to attend the seminars, read the books, and utilize all resources you have designated as pertinent to attaining your goals.

- Identify new mentors who could help you in these subject areas and revisit your mentor exercise.

- Record all of the above.

EXAMPLE: YOUR PERSONAL DEVELOPMENT

SUBJECT	RESOURCES	METHOD	TIME	WHY
Effective Speaking & Human Relations	Dale Carnegie	Class instruction	1981	Present oneself professionally.
Management Skills	Dale Carnegie	Class instruction	1987	Provide teachings on managing staff.
Creativity & Innovation Studies	Dale Carnegie	Class instruction	1988	Think out of the box & creative problem solving.
Best Business Practices	FMI Quaker Executive	3 weeks of sessions	1988	Become well balanced executive.
Negotiations	Hunt Wesson	In-person seminar	1989	Learn to reach agreements in a win-win fashion.
Category Management	Retail Work Process	Class instruction	1993 1994	Learn world class method of conducting business.
Leader in the Class	Dale Carnegie	Class instruction	1989	Skills that assist me in managing my team.
The Signature Cell Healing	Fred Sterling	3 day workshop	2010 2012	Learn alternative methods to healing ones body.
Real Estate Business Models	Robert Kiyosaki	3 day workshop	2009 2010	Real estate investment knowledge & expertise
Self Publishing	Gerry Robert	3 day conference	2013 2015	Learn how to publish my books.
Social Media	TBD	Online course	Future	Learn effective social media marketing approaches
Web-based Selling	TBD	E-learning modules	Future	Learn web-based product selling

YOUR PERSONAL DEVELOPMENT

SUBJECT	RESOURCES	METHOD	TIME	WHY

www.achievingsuccesscenter.com

Odyssey of Learning

Creating your own personal "Odyssey of Learning" will expand your network of resources for both traditional and non-traditional learnings that will influence your success in life. One's personal "Odyssey of Learning," which is the pursuit for "Achieving Universal Wisdom", continues to be one of the most rewarding parts of life. In fact, my next book that is in progress, is dedicated to understanding how to achieve universal wisdom and the use of alternative learning methods. These methods will be described in my next book titled, Achieving Universal Wisdom.

Your odyssey of learning can be as simple as attendance at a workshop or as complex as you choose. You have control over the amount of time you apply to learning new concepts, the amount of energy you expend and the financial commitment you budget for your pursuit of higher learnings. The journey can be domestic and/or international. The journey can be scheduled meetings one-on-one with key individuals or they can be presentations, seminars and workshops on selected subjects which you are interested in. They can be with famous people or relatively unknown people. As long as each encounter offers you a significant level of new learning, that is designed to educate, motivate and inspire.

This list is to provide some direction in your quest for your own personal odyssey of learning.

1. Identify areas of interest or of weaknesses that you would like to improve upon.

2. Purchase resources focused on those areas.

3. Research local continuing education classes that are available to you.

4. Attend community events and participate in social organizations related to subject area.

5. Consider online course studies.

6. Check area chamber of commerce's and local event calendars for speakers, events and other activities focused in your areas of interest.

7. Seek out mentors who can assist in your personal growth.

8. Network with area resources.

9. Check for interesting speakers at local colleges and universities.

To help motivate you into action, let me share a few examples of my personal odyssey of learning.

Dalai Lama comes to Buffalo, NY

In September 2006, the Dalai Lama came to Buffalo, New York, as a distinguished speaker at our University. He only visited two cities in the USA that year and Buffalo happened to be one of them. Talk about opportunities of enlightenment. This global, spiritual leader shared his philosophy of love and forgiveness to a packed university and I considered this another highlight to my odyssey of learnings. The Dalai Lama is revered as a significant spiritual leader who is a role model of peace and positive energy.

Gandhi in India

In June 2007, while working with a business client in India, I found time to travel to Ahmedabad, India to visit the home/museum of Mohandas Gandhi, known as Mahatma (the "Great Soul"). He was one of my role models because of his ability to change the rules of engagement by resisting and breaking the British Empire's ownership over the country of India. Gandhi was instrumental in the struggle to free the people of India from the suppressive rule of the British Empire.

I visited Gandhi's home, which has been turned into a museum, and holds his 13 simple possessions he kept in life. He truly lived the life he preached. The significant learnings from this part of my journey were Gandhi's 12 lessons of life. As you read each lesson, you expand your knowledge and reveal new clouds of unknowing.

The Titles of these 12 Lessons are:

Lesson 1	*Truth and Truthfulness*
Lesson 2	*Truth and Confession*
Lesson 3	*Forgiveness: An Act of Nonviolence*
Lesson 4	*Self suffering as an act of Nonviolence*
Lesson 5	*Simple life*
Lesson 6	*Inter-religious relations*
Lesson 7	*Punctuality*
Lesson 8	*Fearlessness*
Lesson 9	*Cleanliness*
Lesson 10	*Preach what you practice*
Lesson 11	*Non-possession (Sharing of wealth)*
Lesson 12	*Service*

I respect that I was fortunate enough to be in India for business which afforded me this opportunity. Regardless of where you are, there will be opportunities for your odyssey of learning all around you. Are you ready and willing to seize these opportunities with passion and commitment? Do not accept any self-imposed limitations that will hinder your journey. Recognize opportunities, seek out new knowledge, and commit to your odyssey of learning.

Gandhi's Grandson comes to Buffalo, NY

In 2012, Arun Gandhi, the grandson of Mohandas Gandhi, came to my hometown of Buffalo, New York for a one day presentation. I was among 200 people who seized this opportunity to learn from Gandhi's grandson. What was amazing, and certainly a highlight to this odyssey of learning, is that I was in the presence of an ancestor of Mohandas Gandhi who knew him in the flesh. Arun lived with his grandfather for a period of time to learn from him. Being among this enriched individual who received first hand learning from Mohandas was a remarkable opportunity.

His grandson was a living library of knowledge in which he shared many of Gandhi's teachings about non-violence and peace within communities. Stories that Arun shared about his grandfather brought to life this legendary person, distinguishing him from other renowned individuals in the history books.

The lessons learned from this lecture have significantly impacted my cloud of unknowing. This was a good example of awakening to the odyssey of learning and seizing opportunities that will enlighten you.

Al Gore at the Lake Chautauqua Institute

In 2008 at the Lake Chautauqua Institute in Chautauqua, New York, former Vice President Al Gore spoke on global warming. Global warming is of great concern considering the future of our children will be directly impacted by the disruption of nature's harmony and balance. Fortunately, the Institute is within driving distance from Buffalo, NY which allowed my wife and me to take advantage of this opportunity.

This gave us a chance to learn about global warming and as always, we recognized the "cloud of unknowing". We learned things we didn't know, we didn't know! That is the magic about the odyssey of learning, you go there to learn about one of your interests and in addition you end up learning about subjects beyond what you expected. This in turn, adds growth to your understanding of life, the universe, and critical issues that affect all of us globally. Another positive step in my journey.

Rene May in Culiacan, Mexico

In May, 2011, while working with a client in Culiacan, Mexico, I had the opportunity to meet René May, a spiritual healer, and participate in one of his meditation workshops. I have tried to allocate more time to different forms of meditation to increase my access to achieving universal wisdom and to mastering the Mayan 13 day learning cycle.

René May had perfected a healing meditation that had touched hundreds of people in Mexico. As a student of Rene May, I learned many positive energy/mediation concepts and a particular breathing technique. I would not have experienced and learned from a renowned teacher if it weren't for my passion to pursue my "odyssey of learning".

The odyssey of learning is one means for each of us to have the ability to open doors to new learnings and then combine this new information with your present understanding of that particular subject. When you do this, you elevate your insights and understanding of the true realities of life and advance towards achieving your life success plan.

Life should not only be lived, it should be celebrated.
~ Osho, Indian Mystic, Guru & Teacher

Celebrate Your Achievements

Whenever you reach a goal or meet an objective you should celebrate it. Why? When you celebrate your success you are reconfirming with positive energy your accomplishment, and as previously stated, this positive energy will attract more positive results. This positive affirmation is training your mindset to reinforce that you are "successful," which will translate into more positive outcomes. Each time you reach a goal, celebrate in some small way.

When you reach a big goal—one of your ten year goals, for example—you deserve a special recognition. Think about something you would like to do that lives up to your achievement. Plan a night away with your spouse or friend, have dinner at your favorite restaurant, or some type of recognition as a reward. Positive energy breeds positive results.

In my case, I was proud to have reached twenty years of marriage with my lovely wife. In today's world of relationships, this definitely is an accomplishment to celebrate. For our twentieth wedding anniversary we celebrated by taking the family to Hawaii for the first time. It was a goal we set for our ten-year anniversary but didn't reach. We were persistent in our goal and ten years later it finally paid off. In addition to the trip, my wife bought me a 200-pound amethyst gem tower relic as an anniversary gift. She knew I wanted something significant to symbolize our twenty years of devotion and faithfulness to each other. It serves as a great reminder every day to celebrate our success in marriage.

It's important to share your accomplishments with others and celebrate with those who may have been instrumental in your success, especially if they were your past or current mentors. Also, remember the importance of gratitude, it generates positive energy and increases your ability for future success. Use this powerful tool by recognizing those who contributed to your success. You can never do enough of this.

Your choice of celebration may differ with each accomplishment. It's not the financial commitment to your celebrations, it's the validation of your successes that provide the positive energies that will encourage you to continue to reach your short-term and long-term goals.

As important as it is to celebrate your own victories, it is equally as important to celebrate achievements by others. This could mean joining in at the office party for a co-worker who was promoted or special recognition when your son or daughter wins an award. Celebrating achievements is about positive accolades reinforcing the journey of success.

TAKEAWAYS: Odyssey of Learning

- Creating your own personal "Odyssey of Learning" will expand your network of key individuals who can influence your success in life.

- Be prepared to recognize and take advantage of opportunities to learn as they occur.

- The level of commitment to the odyssey of learning will influence the degree of your success.

TAKEAWAYS: Celebration

- Always celebrate your short and long-term goals to motivate your continued progress towards achieving your dreams of success.

Conclusion

Congratulations! You have completed the 7 Step Process for developing your own personal life success plan. This is a big accomplishment and one you should be proud of.

Now the real work begins. Your challenge is to walk the talk, which means, you need to start to embrace and incorporate the many new learnings that you have read or completed in the exercises. With your written life success plan document in hand, you now have a strategic advantage in your life and are more likely to accomplish the goals as documented.

These written exercises that you have completed are very powerful tools. What makes your written document even more powerful is when you declare your intentions and share your plans with others, thus raising your positive energies through collective consciousness. The more people sharing in your energies, the more positive energies are exerted for your success. Collective consciousness is a concept that is discussed at length in my next book, "Achieving Universal Wisdom".

We sincerely wish you good luck on your journey and would appreciate hearing about your success stories. You can share them with us by emailing at **achievingsuccesscenter@gmail.com.**

Always remember, success is not an end in itself. It's an ongoing cycle in your journey of life. Good Luck!

Enjoy the Journey!

KEY ACTION STEPS

A Checklist for Success in Your Life and Career

If you are not attaining the levels of success that you envision yourself reaching, you may find it useful to review the following list of key actions steps which are discussed at length in this book.

1. Define what success means to you based on your personal dreams.

2. Record your path of life, outlining the highs and lows you have encountered along the way.

3. Document your observations and implications of what you have experienced.

4. Define your strengths, weaknesses, opportunities, and threats (SWOT).

5. Set long-term ten year goals and short-term 1 year goals. Be very specific and detailed.

6. Learn how to manage your time effectively and balance your life by setting monthly, weekly and daily priorities.

7. Write a personal mission statement for yourself.

8. Use positive attitudes and disciplines in your life. Include the positive tool of gratitude.

9. Don't blame others, accept responsibility for your life.

10. Master the art of getting past life's barriers; inconveniences versus problems.

11. Visualize reaching your goals with specific details and including all of your senses.

12. Seek out mentors in your life to become enlightened with the Cloud of Unknowing. Think about who your roles models are in life.

13. Maintain a plan for ongoing personal growth development.

14. Create your own "Odyssey of Learning".

15. Celebrate your achievements.

ABOUT THE AUTHOR

Michael Coppola
Former CEO of Advanced Auto Parts

I have known Dennis for over 30 years, going back to when he first became a buyer for the regional supermarket chain where we both worked. We worked together over a ten year period of exponential transformation and sales growth and I had the pleasure of being both his indirect and direct superior during that time but most importantly maintained a mentor and teacher student relationship. Our work consisted of the strategic planning and designing--based on solid merchant focus on the customers' wants and needs and opening supermarkets with the customer as the focus of the design. Of course much of our focus was on the tactical day to day merchandising and operations needed to satisfy and attract the customer and support the store and the store teams. When Dennis left the company after ten years in that role he pursued the next ten year plan of his career in international business consulting. Dennis and I have continued our friendship and business relationship, and sharing of our learning experiences throughout these past 30 years.

Since I have known Dennis, he has impressed me as a continuous student, always looking to expand his base of understanding and knowledge of many different subjects in life. I have observed, as well as participated in at times, his ongoing odyssey of learning over the years. As much as Dennis enjoys teaching at his seminar/workshops and with his consulting clients, he remains committed to learning from all his daily life and work experiences. Dennis practices his new learnings and beliefs both in his career and family life. Let me share three of the principles found in his book that I have seen Dennis embrace regularly.

There is no better example than Dennis' ten year plans highlighted in step 3. His life has been a series of ten year plans with goals, both in relation to his personal life and career ladder. As his superior and mentor, I knew that Dennis' goals were for both the company and himself, both short term and long term. Dennis had everything committed to writing so that he never lost focus on every part of his plans. Therefore, when Dennis met his career goals with our company and left to pursue his next ten year goals, he did so with a commitment to his next strategic ten year plan. Even today, as our friendship and relationship has continued, he keeps me abreast of his strategic life plans which include the launching of his three new books through which he hopes to create a global brand. Dennis conscientiously incorporates within his life the elements he teaches as living proof of their effectiveness in achieving life and career success.

In step 6, you will find an example of how Dennis emphasizes learning from mentors, which in fact is how our relationship developed. When Dennis accepted the position as buyer within our company, he became my indirect subordinate at that time. I recognized early on that Dennis was absorbing much of my expertise about marketing and merchandising--much as I did from my mentors. My role became mentor to Dennis, who hence considered himself the student. When Dennis became a department assistant director, I then became his direct boss. I knew Dennis was passionate about excelling and growing to the position as director of the grocery department, however he lacked the essential skills, knowledge and experience to hold that position. Dennis recognized this and opened himself up in order to expedite his personal and career growth within the company. I made the commitment to work with Dennis both as his boss and his mentor to teach him the necessary skills and expose him to all facets required to shape him into the leader needed to become director. At times, the learning curve was challenging for Dennis but his positive attitude helped him believe this could be accomplished and kept him focused on learning all aspects of the supermarket business.

A mentor can only expand the knowledge base of a student if that individual is teachable, someone with passion and conviction. Dennis displayed self-initiative, and as his mentor, I opened doors to his odyssey of learning because of this positive attitude to excel. Dennis explains the importance of attitudes, gratitude, and disciplines in step 4, which reminds me that these were his key components as he continued to move up the career ladder. In this step, Dennis refers to a sign that he hung on the wall in his office for his team to read, in an effort to instill positive attitudes that drive a successful department and company. Many people can learn from the effectiveness of positive attitudes, gratitude, and disciplines.

As much as both Dennis and I travel, we visit a couple of times each year maintaining our ongoing friendship and continuing the mentor-student relationship which has become a lifetime commitment. Our relationship has been mutually enjoyable and beneficial.

Michael Coppola

DENNIS' PROFILE

Dennis Sobotka is an International Business Consultant, Success Mentor, and International Speaker with his company, Your Partner in Business (YPIB), located in Buffalo, NY, USA. He has been a global business consultant for the past twenty years and his client base includes retailers, suppliers and public & social organizations.

Dennis started his business career in management at TOPS Supermarkets, Inc., A Division of Ahold. His 17 years of experience at TOPS included positions as store manager, procurement buyer, merchandising staff coordinator, and director of grocery department with one billion in sales. Dennis' work included the design and implementation of Category Management; responsible for Store Design/Layout; experience in all line retail functions (store operations, procurement and merchandising, and logistics); experience in a wide range of ECR based initiatives (Electronic Data Interchange, Continuous Replenishment and Quick Response, supplier multi-functional team collaboration). Dennis is a graduate of the State University College at Buffalo with a B.S. in Business Studies, Marketing and Sales.

Dennis has been in the field of Business Consulting since 1994. Dennis was a managing partner for the consulting firm, The Partnering Group, from 1994 to 2001. Dennis then formed his own business consulting firm, Your Partner in Business, in 2001. His consulting work has delivered significant results with multi-format retailers and suppliers around the world. His work focuses on strategic vision, action plans, multi-format store design, business best practices, category management and implementation. He is one of the international leaders in the development of Next Generation Store Design based on the creation of strategic competitive advantages. His store design work has taken hold in South America, South Africa, India, Europe, China, Canada, Mexico and the United States. Dennis provides his clients with strategic direction to build new stores around their strategic category business plans. This process assists retailers in reinventing their retail format to reflect consumer needs and strategic category roles. Dennis' success is his philosophy of delivering results and value to his clients. He is also authoring a book titled, "Achieving Business Success."

In addition to his consulting work, Dennis has been presenting Business and Success Seminars globally to diverse audiences, including senior executives and middle management in retailer and supplier companies; students and underprivileged youth in social organizations; paroles in halfway houses; male and female prisoners residing in correctional facilities; underprivileged adults in labor ready companies; and members of social organizations. Dennis' Success Planning Seminars are tailored to meet the needs of these various audiences. This book, "Achieving Life and Career Success" is based on Dennis' seminars however contains additional information beyond that which is presented at the seminars. Dennis' interest and passion is helping each individual to get past life's barriers and assist them in achieving their full potential for success.

He is married to his wife Patricia of 39 years and they have 3 adult children. He has traveled the world with his family and continues to be an integral part of their lives. His interests include outdoor activities, traveling, physical sports, and his odyssey of learning. Dennis will always be a student first, and then teacher, as he thrives on increasing his knowledge in all areas of his life and career.

Dennis' passion is his odyssey of learning by exploring, discovering, understanding, and incorporating universal wisdom into his daily life. This odyssey of learning is the subject of another of Dennis' book titled, "Achieving Universal Wisdom." His intent is to awaken individuals to their untapped universal potential and provide them with alternative means of learning. He offers his readers non-traditional methodologies that stimulate their conscious and subconscious self toward achieving higher awareness and usage of their universal energies.

Achieving Life & Career Success Set (Now Available)

The magic of Dennis' book is the 7 step process that provides a specific step-by-step method to create your own customized written life success plan. This personalized success plan is unique and powerful with results that have delivered significant life and career changes.

The Achieving Life & Career Success Set consists of the original book, 8.5x11 workbook and condensed 8.5x11 success plan booklet. These products can be used by individuals or groups interested in using the correct tools to define and achieve their success. Sponsorship of these products by companies or organizations can increase their recognition and involvement in their community.

www.achievingsuccesscenter.com

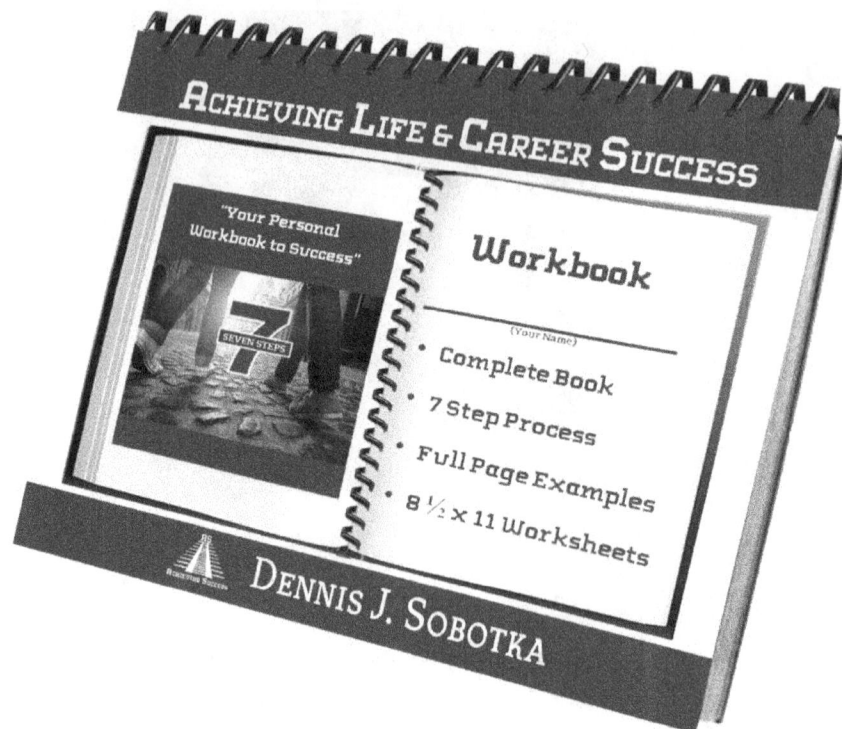

Workbook (Now Available)

The Achieving Life & Career Success Workbook is a combination book and workbook. First it contains the original Achieving Life & Career Success book with the 7 step process for success. Second, the workbook takes you step by step through the text reading followed by the exercise workshops. It provides you with completed 8.5x11 worksheet examples and blank worksheet to assist you in completing the exercises. These worksheets can be used in conjunction with the book, as well as those presented at the Achieving Life & Career Success seminars and classroom instructions. The completed worksheets will reflect each individual's own defined plan for success in their life following the 7 step process. This workbook is effective for both individuals and in a group or classroom setting as it is complete and ready to be used.

www.achievingsuccesscenter.com

Success Plan Booklet (Now Available)

The Success Plan is a personalized booklet consisting of blank worksheets that correspond to the exercises taught in the Achieving Life & Career Success book, workbook and seminar workshops. When used in conjunction with the book, workbook or seminar, the completed booklet offers you a condensed summary of your own personalized success plan. It can then be easily shared with spouses, family, friends, coaches, teachers, and special people in your life.

www.achievingsuccesscenter.com

Products & Services:

ACHIEVING
LIFE & CAREER SUCCESS

PRODUCTS:
- Paperback/Hard Cover/eBook: "Achieving Life & Career Success"
- Workbook: "Achieving Life & Career Success"
- Success Plan Booklet: "Your Success Plan"
- DVD: Seven Step Process to Success

SERVICES:
- Seminar/Workshops: 5, 6, 7, 8 hrs. or Customized
- Seminar/Workshops: 2 Days
- Seminar/Workshops: Organizational Retreats

SPONSORSHIP for Community Groups:
- Provide Books & Workbooks to Organizations (Class Set)
- Present On-site Seminars with Books & Workshops
- Ongoing Mentorship Support

INTERNATIONAL SPEAKER:
- Seven Step Process to Achieving Success
- Visualization: The Magical Tool
- Odyssey of Learning
- Customized Presentations

MENTORSHIP:
- One on One Coaching
- Group Coaching
- Organizational Coaching

Available 2016 / 2017   **Available 2016 / 2017**

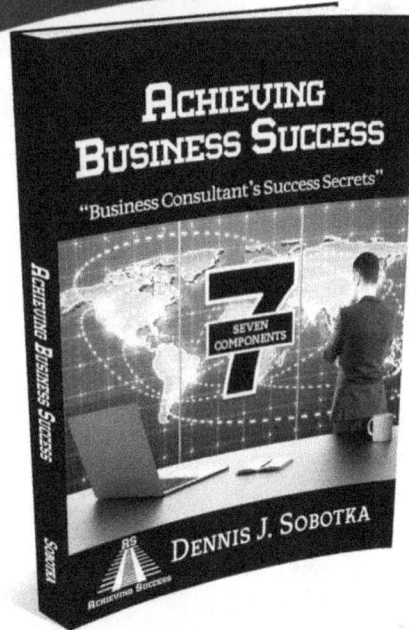

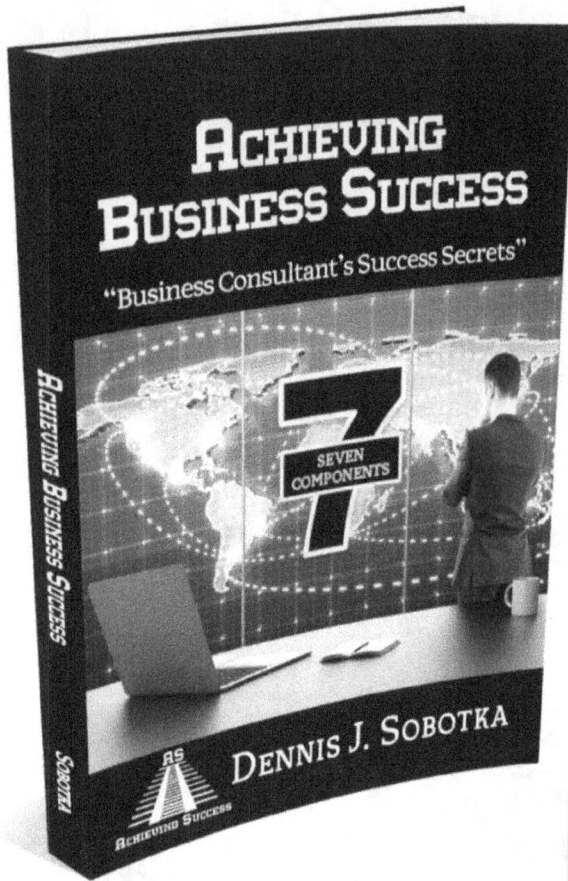

**Available
2016/2017**

"Let's Take This Journey Together"

Dennis' global expertise with retailers and suppliers provides you with proven business best practices that will ensure deliverables. The 7 components presented in this book reflects success secrets which can be incorporated into your individual business situation. Dennis has delivered value and results globally using these 7 components.

SEVEN COMPONENTS TO SUCCESS

1. **Strategic Vision**
2. **Marketing Strategy**
3. **Best Practices**
4. **Innovation & Change**
5. **Strategic Competitive Advantage**
6. **People & Culture**
7. **Tactical Implementation**

DENNIS J. SOBOTKA   *AchievingSuccessCenter.com*

Dennis Sobotka is an International Business Consultant, Success Mentor, Author, and International Speaker with his company, Your Partner in Business (YPIB), and Achieving Success (AS), located in Buffalo, NY, USA.

Products & Services:

ACHIEVING
BUSINESS SUCCESS

PRODUCTS:
- Paperback Book: "Achieving Business Success"
- Hard Cover Book: "Achieving Business Success"
- eBook: "Achieving Business Success"

BUSINESS CONSULTING SERVICES:
- Capability Assessment and Recommendations
- Category Management: Understanding & Application
- Consumer Driven Strategic Business Development
- Strategic Long Term Planning
- Strategic Category Business Development & Implementation
- Strategic Competitive Advantage Development
- Next Generation Store Design for Strategic Success
- Multi-Format Development to Capture Maximum Market Share
- Cluster Marketing and Centers of Excellence
- Human Resources: Developing Successful People

INTERNATIONAL SPEAKER:
- Category Management
- Strategic Competitive Advantage Development
- Cluster Marketing: Centers of Excellence
- Next Generation Store Design / Multi Formats
- Multi-Format Overview
- Strategic Long Term Planning

MENTORSHIP:
- One on One Coaching

ACHIEVING UNIVERSAL WISDOM

"Reach Your Full Potential"

SEVEN LEVELS 7

DENNIS J. SOBOTKA

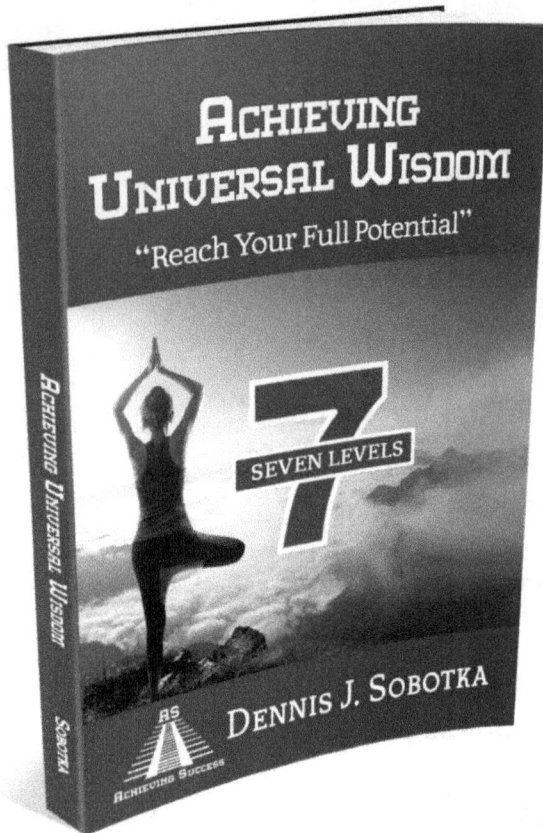

Available 2016/2017

"Let's Take This Journey Together"

Dennis' mystic understanding of the 7 levels of Achieving Universal Wisdom is reflected in this book's collection of breakthrough learnings. He focuses his teachings on helping individuals activate their personal energy sources to master each of the 7 levels of wisdom. The ultimate quest is to "Achieve Your Full Potential!"

SEVEN LEVELS OF UNIVERSAL WISDOM

1. Stuck In the Mud
2. Stepping Up
3. Stepping Out
4. Crossing the Line
5. Crossing the Bridge
6. Entering The Portal
7. Multi-Dimensions

DENNIS J. SOBOTKA

AchievingSuccessCenter.com

Dennis Sobotka is an International Business Consultant, Success Mentor, Author, and International Speaker with his company, Your Partner in Business (YPIB), and Achieving Success (AS), located in Buffalo, NY, USA.

Products & Services:

ACHIEVING
UNIVERSAL WISDOM

PRODUCTS:
- Paperback Book: "Achieving Universal Wisdom"
- Hard Cover Book: "Achieving Universal Wisdom"
- eBook: "Achieving Universal Wisdom"

SERVICES:
- Seminar/Workshops: 2, 4, 6, 8 hrs. or Customized
- Seminar/Workshops: 2 Days
- Seminar/Workshops: Organizational Retreats

SPEAKER: Achieving Full Potential:
- Seven Levels to Achieving Universal Wisdom
- The Odyssey of Learning
- Life Long Learning Tools
- Universal Time verses Man Made Time
- 12-12-12 Chakras, Auras, Dimensions
- Connecting the Dots for Reality/ Wisdom

SPEAKER: Understanding Reality:
- Peak of the American Empire
- The Matrix — Americans Live In
- Who is They — One World Government
- History of People Control
- Enslavement of America
- American History: Redefining 250 years

MENTORSHIP:
- One on One Coaching

DENNIS SOBOTKA

Business Consultant
Author / Speaker
Success Mentor

BUSINESS CONSULTANT

Your Partner In Business

The Partnering Group, Inc.

DIRECTOR of GROCERY

Tops Markets

SUCCESS MENTOR

Achieving Success

Caring Hands

INTERNATIONAL SPEAKER

China; India; Europe; South Africa; Mexico;
South America; Japan; United Kingdom;
Jamaica; Bermuda; Canada; United States

Website: www.achievingsuccesscenter.com

Email: achievingsuccesscenter@gmail.com

REFERENCES

Pillay, S.; (2009). *The Science of Visualization: Maximizing Your Brain's Potential During The Recession,* Huffpost Healthy Living

Merriam-Webster Online Dictionary copyright © 2015 by Merriam-Webster, Incorporated

Gawain, S. (1978). *Creative Visualization,* by Shakti Gawain Paperback

Matthews, G, (2013). *Five Ways to Make New Year's Resolutions Stick.* Forbes 2013

Biography.com Editors, (2015). *O.J. Simpson Biography,* A&E Television Networks, http://www.biography.com/people/oj-simpson-9484729

O'Connell, J. (1996). *Are You Afraid of Success,* Fortune Magazine

Brandon, N. (1999). *The Art of Living Consciously,* Touchstone Publishers

Oxford Dictionary, (2015). Oxford University Press. http://www.oxforddictionaries.com

Miller, D. (2015). *Write Yourself a Check,* CBN.com, The Christian Broadcasting Network, Inc.

Wikipedia, (2015), *Creative Commons Attribution-ShareAlike,* Wikimedia Foundation, Inc.

Litman, L. (2015). *Carli Lloyd had a vision she'd score four goals in the World Cup final.* USA Today Sports

www.ingramcontent.com/pod-product-compliance
Lightning Source LLC
Chambersburg PA
CBHW080556220326
41599CB00032B/6498